David Woodman re-evaluates the importance of Inuit oral traditions in his search to reconstruct the events surrounding Sir John Franklin's tragic 1845 expedition. He shows that previously misunderstood tales of white men travelling through Inuit lands may in fact refer to survivors of the Franklin expedition.

In 1868 American explorer Charles Francis Hall interviewed several Inuit hunters who spoke of strangers travelling through their land. Hall immediately assumed that the hunters were talking about survivors of the Franklin expedition and set off for the Melville Peninsula, the location of many of the sightings, to collect further evidence to support his supposition. His theory, however, was roundly dismissed by historians of his day, who concluded that the Inuit were referring to other white explorers, despite significant discrepancies between the Inuit evidence and the records of other expeditions.

In *Strangers Among Us* Woodman re-examines the Inuit tales in light of modern scholarship and concludes that Hall's initial conclusions are supported by the details of the Inuit remembrances, remembrances that cannot be explained by reference to other expeditions but are consistent with the Franklin expedition.

DAVID C. WOODMAN is assistant harbour master, Prince Rupert, British Columbia.

McGill-Queen's Native and Northern Series
Bruce G. Trigger, Editor

Strangers Among Us

DAVID WOODMAN

McGill-Queen's University Press
Montreal & Kingston • London • Buffalo

© McGill-Queen's University Press 1995
ISBN 0-7735-1348-5

Legal deposit third quarter 1996
Bibliothèque nationale du Québec

Printed in Canada on acid-free paper
McGill-Queen's University Press is grateful to
the Canada Council for support of its
publishing program.

Canadian Cataloguing in Publication Data

Woodman, David C. (David Charles), 1956–
Strangers among us

(McGill-Queen's native and northern studies
series, ISSN 1181-7453; 10)
Includes bibliographical references and index.
ISBN 0-7735-1348-5

1. Franklin, John, Sir, 1786–1847.
2. Arctic regions – Discovery and exploration –
British.   3. Melville Peninsula (N.W.T.) –
History.   4. Inuit – Northwest Territories.
I. Title.   II. Series.

FC3961.3.W66 1995   917.19′5041′0922
C95-900539-0   G660.W66 1995

This book was typeset by
Typo Litho composition inc.
in 10.5 / 13 Palatino

For my parents

Contents

Maps and Illustrations

Author's Note

The aboriginal inhabitants of Canada's Arctic are properly called Inuit ("the people"), and this usage is followed throughout the text except in quoted material in which various forms (Esquimaux, Innuits, etc.) are found. To the Inuit, all non-Inuit were either Etkerlin (Indians) or kobluna, which has been translated somewhat inexactly as "white men." (The Inuit were familiar with racial variation among kobluna; when they encountered negro whalers, they called them "black kobluna.") According to Inuit traditions, all non-Inuit were the descendants of a disobedient Inuit girl and a dog.

Place names from the last century occasionally offer problems. King William Island, although known to be insular, retained its former name of King William's Land for many years, and Hall used it in this form. I have intentionally used some anachronistic names: Amitoke, Great Fish River, and Parry Bay. The first is now the Amitioke Peninsula, while the the second is the Back River, named after Sir George Back. The bay known to Rae and Hall as Parry Bay is now called Franklin Bay. Since most of the testimony involved here uses these old names, I have also done so in the text to avoid confusion or tiresome correction. It should be noted that Hall occasionally referred to Parry Bay as Monumental Inlet.

Hall's writing and spelling styles were idiosyncratic and not very consistent. This is especially true of Inuit names and terms, which he tended to alter as his ear became more attuned to the subtleties of the language. Common examples are the names Quasha (also Quasher, Quashu), Tooshooarthariu (he often dropped the last "i" and occasionally shortened the name to "Tu"), and Aglooka (Eglooka). The reader should be able to follow the various permutations, but when doubt exists I have included the most common form in parentheses.

To assist in the understanding of unfamiliar Inuit names and terms, I have included a glossary (see appendix). Note that this is not intended to be taken as linguistically sound; it is solely a guide to Hall's (and occasionally Sir William Parry's or John Rae's) usage. Translations of terms generally follow those of Knud Rasmussen.

Preface

In 1991 I published *Unravelling the Franklin Mystery: Inuit Testimony*, which attempted to piece together the tragic series of events concerning the disaster that befell the Franklin expedition of 1845. My method was to re-examine the scarce physical evidence that had been recovered, in the light of native traditions and recollections concerning strange white men in the Arctic. During my research for that book, I was led to the papers and journals of Charles Francis Hall. Hall had lived with the Inuit of the central Arctic from 1864 to 1869 and had collected a prodigious number of Inuit folk stories about white men. These stories fell into two categories: those that could easily be attributed to expeditions known to have penetrated the area – led by Sir William Parry (1821–23), Sir John Ross (1829–34), and John Rae (1846–47 and 1854) – and those dealing with the activities of "unknown" white men.

Many of the stories of strangers centred around King William Island, the site of the Franklin disaster, and I felt that most of them could reasonably be attributed to the activities of Franklin's men. A second major group of stories dealt with the presence of strangers on and near the Melville Peninsula, farther east. Hall believed that this second group of tales also concerned Franklin survivors. This conclusion was ridiculed at the time and has not gained very much support from more recent historians. For the sake of completeness, I had originally included the Melville Peninsula stories in my book on

Franklin, even though I tended to agree that they were not remembrances of Franklin's men. But as the book approached publication, the publisher wisely decided that this peripheral portion could safely be excised from what had turned into an overlong and poorly focused work. Yet the "Kia stories" stayed with me.

After publication of the Franklin book, while engaged in the promotion and publicity, I was commonly asked my opinion about where the last few stragglers of Franklin's crew had finally succumbed. In that book I had followed the trail of evidence to "Starvation Cove" on the northern coast of the Adelaide Peninsula and had concluded that a few men (probably less than ten) had left that place in the fall of 1851 in an unsuccessful attempt to make their way home. Although this was as far as I thought the evidence could legitimately be carried, it became obvious during the book's promotion that my readers wanted a further resolution to the question. I therefore took to explaining that there were still some unresolved stories dealing with white men farther east in the Melville Peninsula area during the appropriate time frame. Whereupon I was commonly asked, "Why didn't you write about them?" So I have.

Acknowledgments

Although the opinions and errors contained herein are all my own, I did not write this book without assistance. I owe thanks to many more people that it is possible to enumerate here, but some individuals deserve mention. Dr Harold Langley of the Smithsonian Institution was a kind and generous host whose assistance with the intricacies of the Hall Collection was invaluable. Mr Edmund Carpenter brought the Comer manuscript to my attention, and Mrs Dorothy Harley Eber kindly shared some of the material which she had gathered while interviewing Inuit for her work on early whalers. Mr John Bockstoce, Dr Arthur Credland, and W. Gillies Ross freely offered their expertise and support as I attempted to track down any "missing" whalers.

As every author knows, the actual work of production is much more arduous than the writing, and I was once again ably shepherded through this process by Joan McGilvray at McGill-Queen's. Carlotta Lemieux's painstaking editing removed all traces of my sloppy writing and thinking from the final manuscript and made me appear at least twice as intelligent as I really am.

I would like to thank all the participants of the Royal Canadian Geographical Society's 1994 King William Island Expedition who accompanied me to the historic shores that have so dominated my writing life, especially Dr George Hobson and Dr Charles Arnold, whose efforts made the expedition possible.

Finally, I again owe a great debt to my wife Franca and my daughters Natalie and Laura. This book should prove that Daddy wasn't (always) playing computer games when he disappeared into the study.

Strangers Among Us

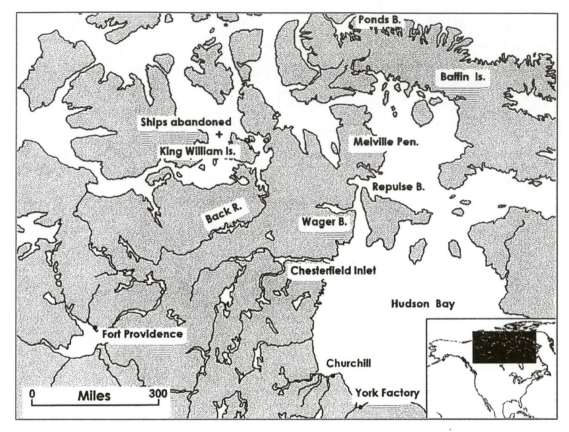

The Central Arctic

Kia and Rae

THE LOST EXPLORERS

In May 1847 Commander James Fitzjames, Captain of HMS *Erebus*, sat in his cabin filling in forms. His ship and HMS *Terror*, both of which were under the overall command of Sir John Franklin, had been locked in the pack ice of Victoria Strait since the preceding September. It was almost two years since the Franklin expedition had left England on a quest to resolve the last small link in the Northwest Passage, yet Fitzjames had no cause for concern.

Despite their precarious position, the members of the expedition had no need to worry as the short Arctic summer of 1847 approached. Although at least three men had died, their vessels were stoutly built and were provisioned for at least another two years. By discovering and sailing down Peel Strait the previous year, they had arrived within reach of their goal. Now, in their ice-locked position north of Cape Felix, the northernmost point of King William Island, they had reached an area of known geography. The elusive Northwest Passage was within their grasp. About twenty miles farther south lay Victory Point. This had been named by James Clark Ross, who had completed his westbound survey there in 1830 during the expedition led by his uncle, Sir John Ross. Sixty miles south of Victory Point was Cape Herschel, where in 1839 a great cairn had been built by the explorers Thomas Simpson and

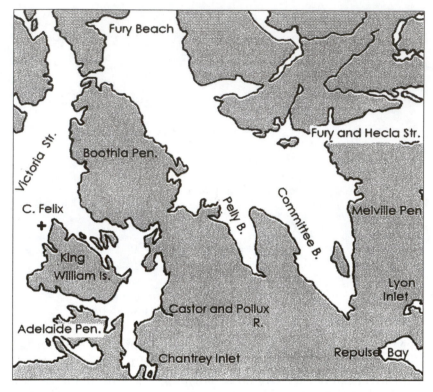

Franklin Area

Peter Warren Dease. Once the land between these two points was surveyed, the dream of centuries – a continuous passage through the Arctic Archipelago – would be realized.[1]

And so, in the gloom of his cabin, Commander Fitzjames filled in the blanks on some preprinted forms. He wrote: "28 of May 1847 H.M.S.hips Erebus and Terror Wintered in the Ice in Lat. 70.5°N Long. 98°.23'w Having wintered in 1846–7 at Beechey Island in Lat 74°.43'.28"N. Long 91°.39'.15"w After having ascended Wellington Channel to Lat 77° and returned by the West-side of Cornwallis Island. Sir John Franklin commanding the Expedition. All well. Party consisting of 2 Officers and 6 Men left the ships on Monday 24th May 1847."[2] The forms were intended to be placed in bottles and periodically dropped over the side, instructions in six languages directing the discoverer to forward them to the British Admiralty. However, the present forms were taken ashore by a small party of men who had been dispatched from the icebound ships to complete the survey of the still unexplored coastline. When completed and signed by the officers in charge of the surveying party (Lieutenant Graham Gore and Mate Charles F. Des Voeux), these forms were soldered into tin canisters and were presumably deposited in places where they were likely to be found.

We do not know how many forms were prepared on that May day, but two were found by later explorers, one at Victory Point and another, essentially identical, a few miles to the south. Later, the Inuit mentioned having found others.[3] Curiously, Fitzjames made the same error on each, for the two ships had wintered at Beechey Island during 1845–46, not 1846–47. This is confirmed by the headstones of the three dead men who were buried there and by a later note, again by Fitzjames, written around the margin of the record found near Victory Point. This addendum tells of the dramatic change that had befallen the expedition's fortunes in the intervening year.

25th April 1848 HM Ships Terror and Erebus were deserted on the 22nd April 5 leagues [about 15 miles] NNW of this having been beset since 12th Sept. 1846. The Officers & Crews consisting of 105 souls under the command of Captain F.R.M. Crozier landed here – in Lat. 69°37′42″ Long. 98°41′ This paper was found by Lt. Irving under the cairn supposed to have been built by Sir James Ross in 1831 [*sic*] – (4 miles to the Northward) – where it had been deposited by the late Commander Gore in June 1847. Sir James Ross' pillar has not however been found and the paper has been transferred to this position which is that in which Sir J Ross pillar was erected – Sir John Franklin died on the 11th June 1847 and the total loss by deaths in the Expedition has been to this date 9 officers & 15 men.[4]

There is evidence that some of these dead officers and men were buried at Cape Felix, where the expedition had established a temporary summer camp in 1847.[5]

Fitzjames had signed himself "Captain HMS Erebus" and passed the note to Franklin's successor as commander of the expedition, Captain Francis Crozier, who had appended his signature, written "Captain and Senior Offr," and added an important postscript: "and start tomorrow, 26th, for Backs Fish River." This note and the scattered trail of skeletons and personal effects that were found along the western shore of King William Island and the adjacent Adelaide Peninsula were the only relics of what became the greatest disaster of Arctic exploration. Crozier, Fitzjames, and their 103 men all perished in their futile march towards civilization.

The Franklin expedition was not the only Arctic exploration undertaken at this time. During the summer of 1847, an explorer named John Rae had been mapping the western coast of Melville Peninsula, 300 miles to the east. One month before Fitzjames wrote the first of the above notes, Rae had traced the shore of Lord Mayor Bay on the eastern side of Boothia Peninsula, unaware that the *Erebus* and *Terror* were in difficulty. At that time Rae had been little more than 100 miles from Franklin's beleaguered ships.

During the next few years, Rae became involved in the massive manhunt that was launched to search for the lost squadron. When this prodigious effort was officially halted in 1854, it had achieved no result beyond the discovery of the aforementioned wintering station on Beechey Island. All hope for the rescue of Franklin and his men was abandoned and the crews were officially proclaimed to have died in March of that year. Rae, released from his part in the Franklin search, was then free to return to Repulse Bay to complete his own coastal survey.

Since various clues had led the authorities to believe that Franklin's expedition had come to grief in the north-central Arctic, Rae felt that there was "no possibility" of finding anything relevant during his planned trip to Repulse Bay. He was thus surprised to become the first white man to learn of the fate of Franklin's men. While westbound in Pelly Bay, through force of habit he asked an Inuit hunter whom he met the standard question about dying white men. The ready answer, simply told, formed the basis of all reconstructions of what had happened to Franklin's doomed expedition:

In the Spring, four winters past, (1850) whilst some Esquimaux families were killing Seals near the north shore of ... King William's Land, about forty white men were seen travelling in company southward over the ice, and dragging a boat and sledges with them. They were passing along the west shore of the above named Island. None of the party could speak the Esquimaux language so well as to be understood, but by signs the Natives were led to believe that the Ship or Ships had been crushed by ice, and that they were then going to where they expected to find deer to shoot. From the appearance of the Men (all of whom with the exception of one Officer, were hauling on the drag ropes of the sledge and were looking thin) – they were then supposed to be getting short of provisions, and they purchased a small Seal or piece of Seal from the natives. The Officer was described as being a tall, stout, middle aged man: When their days journey terminated, they pitched Tents to rest in. At a later date the same Season but previous to the disruption of the ice, the corpses of some thirty persons and some Graves were discovered on the Continent, and five dead bodies on an Island near it, about a long day's journey to the north west of the mouth of a large stream, which can be no other than Backs Great Fish River, (named by the Esquimaux Ook-koo-i-hi-ca-lik) ... Some of the bodies were in a tent or tents; others were under the boat which had been turned over to form a shelter, and some lay scattered about in different directions. Of those seen on the Island, it was supposed that one was that of an Officer, (chief) as he had a telescope strapped over his shoulders, and his double barrelled gun lay underneath him.

From the mutilated state of many of the bodies and the contents of the kettles, it is evident that our wretched Countrymen had been driven to the last dread alternative, as a means of sustaining life. A few of the unfortunate Men must have survived until the arrival of the wild fowl, (say until the end of May,) as shots were heard, and fresh bones and feathers of geese were noticed near the scene of the sad event.[6]

This testimony, which turned out to be amazingly accurate, was confirmed in the most part by discovery of the Victory Point record five years later by Lady Franklin's privately financed expedition commanded by Leopold McClintock.[7] Rae's account, confirmed by McClintock's discovery of scattered campsites and skeletons along the western and southern shores of King William Island, seemed to have resolved the mystery of Franklin's disappearance. Yet one man was unconvinced.

Charles Francis Hall was born in 1821 in Vermont,[8] but little is known of his life until 1849, when he arrived in Cincinatti. He had little formal education, and after apprenticeship to a blacksmith he became a seal engraver, eventually establishing his own business. In 1855 Hall decided to forsake his trade in order to publish a newspaper, the *Cincinnati Occasional*, which started as a single-page publication and slowly grew. It was, however, "a hobby-horse, a mouthpiece for his quirks and special interests," though by 1859 Hall's publishing career had grown to the point that he could distribute a daily paper, the *Daily Press*.[9]

Hall's interests were eclectic, including hot air balloons and Ericsson's caloric engines, both of which threatened to dominate some

Charles Francis Hall
(Smithsonian Institution)

issues of the *Daily Press*. Meanwhile, he married and fathered two children, a daughter born in 1855 and a son five years later, though he rarely mentioned his family in his journals and seems to have found little attraction in domesticity.[10]

Suddenly, in 1857, Hall's wandering if obsessive attention was focused on the Arctic. This may have been inspired by the death of Elisha Kent Kane, a contemporary American veteran of the Franklin search, whose body passed in state through Cincinnati on 7 March 1857 en route to burial in Philadelphia.[11] Throughout this period, Hall filled many notebooks with stray thoughts, ideas, and plans. These notebooks, which had hitherto been a testament to "unfocused but energetic effort in self-education,"[12] now began to deal with details of survival and articles concerning the Arctic. Hall was obsessed with the fate of Franklin's lost expedition, and by 1859 articles about Franklin became a major theme in his newspaper. The same summer that McClintock was searching the shore of King William Island for remains, Hall published a story about four Russian sailors who had been marooned on Spitzbergen for six years with virtually no equipment. These men had adapted to their harsh conditions and, when rescued, were remarkably healthy. "Hall drew the obvious conclusions: so might Franklin and his men have survived and be waiting for rescue."[13]

Hall now felt that he had been "called by God," and he determined to devote the rest of his life to the search for and possible rescue of Franklin survivors. In 1860 he arrived in the Arctic with a small boat and a few provisions. Deposited by friendly whalers on Baffin Island, he hoped to enlist some Inuit guides to take him to the site of the Franklin disaster, but none were enthusiastic to travel so far. When Hall's small boat was wrecked, he reluctantly concluded that there was no chance of reaching King William Island; nevertheless, he spent the next two years living with the Inuit, learning their ways, and enlisting the support of a husband-and-wife team (Ebierbing and Tookoolitoo) as interpreters for another attempt.

In 1864 Hall and his native friends were back. Landing near Wager Bay, they met a small band of Arvilingmiut, who took the strangers to their normal hunting station at Repulse Bay. This was to be Hall's base of operations for the next five years. While there, he spent every available minute interviewing the natives about the fate of the missing Franklin explorers, filling small notebooks with dense and detailed records. Hall believed that much could be learned by assiduously questioning the Inuit, and during his sojourn with the natives of the area he was proved correct.[14]

In most ways the stories the Inuit told Hall between 1864 and 1869 confirmed and enhanced those told to Rae. Hall learned details of the dead men on the island (Todd Islet), and he visited the site to rebury their bones. The natives told of a great death camp at Terror Bay and of some abandoned boats to the north in Erebus Bay. Hall even managed to interview two of the hunters who had met the doomed men on their forlorn march towards civilization.[15]

But some of the testimony that Hall recorded did not fit with the accepted reconstruction of the disaster. The Inuit told of a meeting with the white men on their ships and of a two-year interaction with them, details not found in Fitzjames's addendum. They told of watching one ship sink, of a great caribou hunt during which the white men shot so many animals that their blood made a line across the bay, and of "cemented vaults" where the white men had preserved their records ashore.[16] Most significantly, they told of the final discovery of the second ship many miles to the south in the land of the Ukjulingmiut. They said that the ship was found perfectly preserved in the ice a few miles from the low shore of Ook-soo-see-too near a place called "Shartoo – the flat one." This was the low land on the west coast of the Adelaide Peninsula, ninety miles (as the crow flies) south of Victory Point.

In view of Fitzjames's record that all surviving men had left the ships in a body in 1848, conventional wisdom asserts that this ship was unmanned when found by the Inuit at Shartoo. But the Inuit did not believe this was so. They found "sweepings" near the cabin door of the ship, which led them to believe that white men had recently been living there. Some tales explicitly stated that living white men were seen on board and that for this reason the Inuit delayed their approach until the ship was deserted.[17] Even more conclusively, they found the body of a large white man in a bunk near the stern.[18]

These traditions seemed incompatible with the scenario outlined in the Victory Point record, which stated that all 105 men left both ships intact in the ice in 1848. It was barely conceivable that Fitzjames and Crozier would have left an officer's body aboard when they abandoned the ships; and it was even less likely that this ship had drifted almost one hundred miles in such perfect serenity that deck sweepings on the nearby ice had not been disturbed. Further descriptions rendered such a scenario even more far-fetched, for the natives said the ship was encased in one-year ice and that "a plank was found extending from the ship down on to the ice." The Inuit even discovered "tracks of 4 strangers, not Innuits" on shore nearby.[19]

A native woman named Koowik had lived near the site of the wreck for many years and had heard tell of the sunken ship and the strange tracks. She was familiar with white men, having seen Sir John Ross at Victory Harbour, Dr Rae at Pelly Bay in 1854, and McClintock in 1859. When interviewed by Hall, she not only confirmed that the natives had seen "the tracks of 3 men Kob-loo-nas" but added the interesting detail that there were "those of a dog with them ... The vessel seen 1st & then little while after the tracks of the 3 Kob-lu-nans & dog seen on the land."[20] When the *Erebus* and *Terror* had arrived in the Arctic, there were at least two dogs aboard -"Old Neptune" and an unnamed Newfoundland.[21]

The body aboard the "Ootjoolik" wreck, and the tracks of three or four white men and a dog on the snow nearby remain inconvenient facts which Franklin historians have been hard pressed to assimilate. Hall believed that these men were some of the ones who had abandoned the ships in 1848. He concluded that the vessels had been remanned and that the last few survivors had again abandoned the safety of their vessel at a later date. Even more amazingly, he believed that these men had again been seen by the Inuit while they pursued their lonely march towards safety.

KIA'S TALE[22]

The stories that initially enticed Hall to Melville Peninsula were told by some natives who visited Repulse Bay in 1866. These Inuit told of some strange buildings "not far from Ar-lang-na-zhu & Adge-go" in the northwestern region of the Melville Peninsula. Hall later determined that they had been discovered by a hunter named Koolooa who, according to his friends, "saw the buildings 10 years ago not counting this year or the year that he saw them."[23] Unfortunately, when Hall later met Koolooa, the hunter disclaimed any knowledge of strange buildings, though he said he had seen a strange cairn.[24]

Hall did not place too much belief in these buildings until he interviewed a native named Papa-te-wa (which Hall shortened to Papa) in January 1868. Papa said that the buildings had been found not by Koolooa but by his friend and hunting companion, a young man named Kia, and that Kia had discovered "2 Ig-loos or rather 2 stone buildings."[25] These structures were later described by Kia's sister as being "made of mud or stone." Another of Kia's friends, Kudloon, confirmed that Kia had seen "a stone hut near Ar-lang-na-zhu (Garry Bay) & found in it a piece of canvas. The stone hut was not made by Innuits nor was the canvas anything that the Innuits ever possessed."[26] At this time Hall also heard "about the small [illegible] sled [which] ... was found on one of the Islands of F & H. S. [Fury & Hecla Strait] a few years ago."[27]

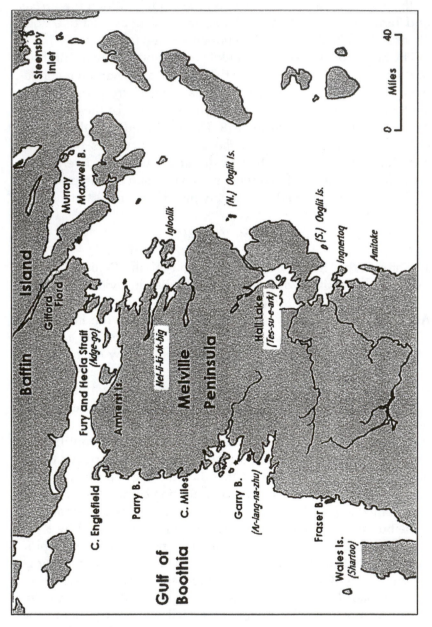

The Melville Peninsula

According to Papa, these structures were "not such as Innuits ever made, but quite large, long, wide, and high."[28] He said they were situated on the southern shore of Fury and Hecla Strait "about half way between Cape Englefield and Amherst Island," which might indicate that they were the remains of temporary structures built by William Parry's men in 1822.[29] Although Hall reserved judgment on the elusive "buildings," he was nevertheless intrigued by the fragmentary stories of their sighting.

In the following weeks, Hall heard other shadowy tales of strange occurrences on or near the Melville Peninsula, including a story that two white men, "one a tall man, the other considerably shorter," had been seen within the last three years.[30] The wives of two native hunters named Ikkumer and Quasha told Hall of two Etkerlin (Indians) who had been seen near the island of Igloolik, which was the site of a semi-permanent village near the northeastern corner of the Melville Peninsula. Captains Parry and Lyon had wintered there in 1822–23, but as far as Hall knew, no white man had approached the place since. Ikkumer's wife persisted in calling the strangers Etkerlin, but Karwonga (Quasha's wife) corrected her, saying, "No, Kobluna" (white man) "at the same time swing[ing] her hands in immitation [sic] of white men swinging their hands [while walking]."[31] Karwonga told of the "long [tall] man forward, short one behind with bundle on his back about 2 feet long" and remarked that they wore dark clothes with big capes on their coats.[32] Hall's informants did not theorize about who these strange white men might be, yet he confidently asserted that "information has finally led me to give the joyful news that white men of Sir John Franklin's Expedition may still be living on the south shore of Fury & Hecla Strait."[33]

Hall decided that a personal visit to the area was justified. Arriving at the South Ooglit Isles in April 1868, he interviewed Kudloon, who recollected "that Qua-shu [Quasha] & his wife Kar-wong-a told him at the time about seeing white men several years ago when they saw the 2 white men at Nel-li-ki-ok-big – a place in the High Land NW of here [Igloolik]."[34] When Hall asked whether their testimony could be relied on, he was told that Quasha would "shay-la-vou (lie) a good deal, but his wife will not tell lies."[35]

While there, Hall again heard the tale of Kia's experience with strangers. It was known to all the Inuit, and although Kia had been killed by a "very ugly walrus" a year after his strange encounter,

Hall was able to interview Kia's companion of that hunting season, Koolooa. Hall learned that at some time in the past, Kia and seven companions[36] had gone caribou hunting with their families on the west coast of Melville Peninsula. They had broken up into smaller units in order to conduct their hunt more successfully. Kia and Koolooa had decided to hunt together and had set off with their families for the extreme northwest corner of the peninsula, while the others hunted farther south at Arlangnazhu (Garry Bay). Koolooa picked up the tale:

Koo-loo-a says at same time he was hunting with Ki-a he had killed a deer & sat himself down on a rock & eat [*sic*] some of the meat. He had put his head down & just before getting his mouth to the water he heard something crack which he says was *ti-ma-na-t* (the same) as the crack of guns. He had heard the crack of guns when living at Too-noo-nee (Ponds Bay). He could not tell from which direction the sound came on account of his position in the act of drinking. Looked about but could see no one & did not hear the noise again. The place was near the N.W. extreme of Melville Peninsula as he (Koo-loo) points out on Parry's Chart. Same day Koo-loo-a heard the crack as he thought of a gun while walking around he came to fresh tracks on some grass & earth the tracks longer than his ... the tracks so fresh that the grass had not all regained their erect position. Some of it (the grass) was then gradually lifting up as it had been before being trod upon. The steps long & foot mark "turning out."[37]

These strange tracks made a great impression on Koolooa, and when he rejoined Kia he found that his friend also had found "a great many human footprints."[38]

Hall was told that the "time of year ... was in the summer of the year – when took-too [caribou] had short hair – no snow on the ground."[39] He was also told that "the tracks were in the sand for it was in the fall when snow was off the ground."[40] The two Inuit hunters were understandably alarmed at these strange tracks, which were completely unlike those made by their own people with their soft-soled boots and characteristic "pigeon-toed" gait. Two days later the strange footprints and the shooting noise were explained:

Next morning after hearing crack & seeing tracks both Koo-loo-a and Ki-a moved their tents & families away from that place – The next morning after moving Koo-loo-a went to work fixing the skin of the deer he had killed. As Koo-loo-a was late in getting ready Ki-a started off deer hunting alone. By & by Ki-a saw a man coming up the hill on which he (Ki-a) was coming directly toward him. Ki-a thought at first the man to be Koo-loo-a but on looking longer & more observingly Ki-a saw his mistake for it was not Koo-loo-a but a strange man having a cap on his head that was distinct from his coat. He saw that he (the stranger) had *strange* clothes on & carried something *strange* in a *strange* way on his shoulder. Ki-a could not from his position behind the rock see much of the stranger's face – the clothes not black nor white – coat on that came down to or *almost* to his knees – the make of clothes altogether different from In-nuits. The stranger had something across his shoulder running diagonally – this something was long & wide at one end & narrow at the other end. He was walking rather fast & going directly toward the point on NW ex. of Melville Peninsula as showed by K. [Koolooa] on Parry's Chart. Ki-a followed the stranger up for some time & looked sharp at him.[41]

Although Kia was, by all accounts, a brave and resourceful hunter, he was not ready to face this alien being alone. His sister later recalled that he was "a young man at the time he saw the stranger & made afraid very easy" and that he told her he was "no man," for he had not been brave enough to confront the stranger.[42] Kia had heard the elders tell of how, long ago, other Etkerlin (Indians) had come from the south, killing and kidnapping, and he was sure that this stranger was trouble.

According to Papa, Kia was "a man who would never lie." He noted that Kia at the time had "close observation of every object in that country" and that he had a specific reason to be cautious, for "his own life had long been in perpetual danger from the relatives of one who had been slain by one of his kinsmen; for, according to Innuit belief, the soul of the slain can never rest until some near relative of the slayer shall pay the debt with his blood."[43]

Kia followed the stranger for some distance, "all the time keeping himself (Ki-a) hid behind rocks & hills."[44] He confirmed that this stranger and others like him had left the tracks he had seen two days before, for he noticed that the stranger "toed-out" when he walked. When Kia later examined the tracks, he found that they were of a very peculiar shape, "long foot & very narrow in the middle … The tracks showed a deep place at the heel – deeper *than anywhere else* – the steps too not very long for the stranger seemed to be looking around to find something – some game perhaps – as he walked along."[45]

When Kia and Koolooa told each other of their amazing experiences, curiosity outweighed fear. The next morning the two hunters moved their tents "to the same place as where Ki-a saw the strange man & there they all saw the strangers tracks which showed a long foot narrow in the middle."[46] Kia's stranger had walked alone, but according to Kudloon (one of the more southerly hunters), shortly after seeing the stranger, Kia and Koolooa had come across the tracks of a party consisting of three men and a dog. Like the solitary walker seen by Kia a few days earlier, this group was "going toward the N.W. extreme of the land south side of Adg-go Fury & Hecla Strait. The dog tracks showed that the dog belonged to the 3 strangers. From the tracks Ki-a thought those who made them carried something heavy. These three (3) men tracks of same character as those of the strange man he had a little while before seen. The sand so dry that it [illegible] out that it did not well show, but Ki-a thought from the size – the length of the tracks that they could not be Innuits."[47]

Within a few days of the sighting of the stranger, Kia and Koolooa completed their hunt and rejoined Kudloon and their other friends: "From there (the place where the tents were – the place where strange man had been seen) Koo-loo-a & Ki-a with their families removed down to Ar-lang-na-zhu (Garry Bay) & they saw nothing more of the kind he (Koo-loo-a) has been describing."[48] None of the other hunters had seen or heard anything strange, and they confirmed that "no one of their number had been anywhere near where the tracks of 3 men & of dog were seen by Ki-a." The hunters "felt at first some what alarmed thinking perhaps they might be Indians or Pelly Bay natives. Ki-a thought when he saw the stranger & found he was not Koo-loo-a that he was an Indian. After all of them had talked the matter all over near Ar-lang-na-zhu most of them thought the man Ki-a had seen must have been a Kod-lu-na (white man) & yet they couldn't tell how it was possible for him to get there."[49]

In discussions with his friends, Kia elaborated on the details of the stranger's manner and dress. The stranger had "a cap & clothes on altogether different from anything he had ever seen ... saw that he had on a coat of a kind of blue color – light blue ... Had on a long coat that came down to his knees & shook very much in the wind."[50] Nuterlik confirmed that Kia had told him the stranger wore "thin clothes – *not skin clothes*."[51]

The stranger had on a Koo-loo-ta (coat) that had a covering for the head but this was thrown back & lying behind the head, & on his head was a cap … The hair must have been very short so short that the cap completely covered it up so that he couldn't see it. The face the side next to him (Ki-a) white not dark like the Innuits. The coat not exactly white nor black – was long coming down almost to the knees. No tail about it – same length all around (Jo & Hannah & Kud-loon think the coat must have been a white one but had got dirty in wearing it same as the flesh side of deer skin – after long use.)[52]

Everyone Hall interviewed knew of Kia's encounter. Each new informant corroborated the stories of the others, and many added further details. A hunter named Innu remarked that Kia had told how the stranger "had a red neck or something red about his neck. This means a rash as Jo [Hall's interpreter Ebierbing] says."[53] Nothing had escaped Kia's notice. He had said that the stranger carried something on his shoulder:

On getting Ar-mou-yer to describe in what way the thing was carried as Ki-a described to him he shows that a strap passed over the right shoulder down & across the front diagonally & thence deflected back under the left arm in just the way white men sling & carry a gun.

That something on the stranger's shoulder did not look anything like a bow & arrows; it was longer than a *pit-ik-zhee* (Innuits *bow*). Ki-a though once in a while near enough to see the stranger's face distinctly if it had been turned around a little but all the time the stranger's back was toward him. The Innuits who heard Ki-a's story such as had seen guns at Ponds Bay & such as had seen guns of Dr Rae's party thought from Ki-a description that the stranger (*Et-ker-lin*) carried a gun on his shoulder.[54]

Kudloon remembered his friend's description of the gun very well. He noted that "its position diagonal. It looked as if a cover of something was on the outside – one end wider than the other." Hall added, "I now ask Kud-loon which end was down of the long thing Ki-a saw on the stranger's back – the *large* end or *small* end? His answer at once comes: 'Large end down.'" Hall continued:

I now show Kud-loon the Illustration of Parry's Narrative of his voyage of 1821–2 & 3 of Western outlet of the Fury & Hecla Strait where 2 men are represented standing with their backs toward the "looker on" one having

The Inuit identified Kia's stranger as looking similar to this illustration of Parry's men.
(William Edward Parry, *Journal of a Second Voyage for the Discovery of a North-West
Passage from the Atlantic to the Pacific,* London, John Murray 1824)

the butt of his gun on the ground & he resting on it while the other stands
erect with his gun slung diagonally across his back, the butt end down.
Kud-loon instantly points his fingers to the latter figure & says *Ti-nee-na-
tu* – that is *"all the same"* was the long thing on the shoulder of the stranger
Ki-a saw.[55]

Every aspect of Kia's tale was thoroughly talked over among the
Inuit. Hall, a tireless interrogator, continued to elicit details. He was
intrigued by these tales of white men walking along the remote
coast. There was little doubt that the Inuit were telling the truth
about their experiences. According to the hunters, Koolooa was "a
man that talks very little but whatever he does say he speaks truth.
Ki-a a very truthful man & was known to all the Innuits as a truth
telling Innuit."[56]

The natives of Ooglit and Iglooik never tired of telling Hall of
Kia's remarkable experience. Hall interviewed Kia's sister Ark-

ootoo,[57] his hunting partners Koolooa[58] and Kudloon,[59] and Armouyer ("Tom Palmer"), Kia's longtime friend.[60] Each time, he was told the same story with almost boring similarity. The incident had been the defining moment of Kia's short life and one of the most memorable events of his generation.

When Kia described the stranger, "all the Innuits who had ever seen a *Kod-lu-na* before said the stranger must have been one – that is a *white man*."[61] Kia's mother agreed; she "had never seen one but had been told all about how they dressed & walked" by those who had lived "a good many years at Too-noo-nee-roo-chuk (Admiralty Inlet)" among the white whalers.[62] When Hall asked his own informants who they thought Kia had seen, they all said "without a dissenting voice that they think he was a white man."[63]

Despite the Inuit unfamiliarity with exact dating, Hall endeavoured to discover when Kia and Koolooa had had their unforgettable experiences. It was universally agreed that the encounter had occurred the year before Kia's untimely death and that the intervening winter had been one of great adversity and strife among the Inuit of Igloolik. Hall had more difficulty obtaining a date, for the Inuit method of determining time consisted almost entirely of recalling a series of significant events in the past, laboriously paging back through a mental yearbook. After fifteen minutes of deliberation, Hall's informants told him that Kia's encounter had occurred *"thirteen years ago last fall."* Which, Hall concluded, "brings it out that it was in *1854* that Ki-a saw what I have not the least doubt was one of Sir John Franklin's men."[64]

In spite of Hall's opinion, few later historians have believed that Kia's stranger was a member of the Franklin expedition. John Rae had been camped at Repulse Bay during 1854, and although he did not approach the Melville Peninsula that year, he had mapped most of its western shore in 1847. Since no other known white explorer had ever approached the area of Kia and Koolooa's encounter with the stranger, historians generally agreed that Rae and his men had been the source of the story and that the encounter took place in 1847.[65]

The Inuit obstinately refused to agree. When Kia's sister Arkootoo was interviewed about the event, she helpfully tied in the chronology to Rae's visit – but she, like the other Inuit, insisted that "it was after Dr Rae saw at I-wil-lik the 2d time – (that is after 1854 the time he & party left there) that Ki-a saw this stranger."[66] However, the historians remained unconvinced by her assertion. They pointed out that Rae had taken no Inuit guides with him on his 1847 survey and that the natives at his base camp in Repulse Bay had no knowledge of his visit to Melville Peninsula. It seemed obvious, therefore, that Kia and Koolooa had simply seen Rae on this journey and that over the intervening fourteen years an error of seven years had crept into the never-exact Inuit time scale.

Hall continued his cross-examination of Kia's sister:

I lifted my foot to show Ar-koo-too the size of my foot having all my feet geer [i.e., gear] on but – when I asked her if the foot print which Ki-a saw was as large as mine. From this comes the news which is interesting, *unexpected* & important that she (Ar-koo-too) once saw & was the one who 1st saw foot prints in the fresh fallen snow, the 1st snow of the fall (of the year) of a strange person this side of Ar-lang-na-zhu (Garry Bay). The tracks long foot – not Innuits tracks – with longer foot than mine – no deep heel print. This was several years before Ki-a saw the stranger – it was before she had any children her oldest (– an adopted boy) 17 to 20 yrs old I should think. This boy who is now in Ig-loo is same age now made out as "Harry" (deceased Shoo-she-ark-nuk's oldest boy) who is 16 or 17. Snow in such condition that it was hard to make out more than that they were not an Innuits & she measured the length of foot mark with her fingers in the usual way Innuit women measure. After that some other Innuits saw tracks of strangers that is they were not Innuit tracks but of some of some [*sic*] other race.[67]

What are we to make of this account of white men's tracks "several years before Kia saw the stranger"? The age of Arkootoo's boy would indicate that she saw the tracks left by Rae's men in 1847 (just over twenty years before her discussion will Hall in 1868). It is interesting that the prints had no heel marks, for we know that Rae preferred heelless Inuit boots or moccasins.[68] On the other hand, it was the unvarying testimony of all that Kia's stranger had left tracks with "a deep place at the heel – deeper than anywhere else." This detail implies that Arkootoo was not merely repeating her brother's testimony but was giving information of a distinct event and that it was the tracks of Rae's party that she saw.

As amazing as it may seem, Arkootoo's testimony is consistent with the other testimony. She saw white men's tracks without a heel before her son was born (that is, in 1848 or earlier), and this was "several years" before her brother Kia saw his stranger (which was after Rae had left from his second, 1854, expedition). So if Arkootoo saw Rae's 1847 tracks, who was Kia's stranger? Hall concluded that the man must have been a survivor of Franklin's crew. Hall did not preserve all the evidence that led him to this conclusion, yet enough remains in his surviving notes to justify this conclusion at least partly.

The eminent Franklin historian R.J. Cyriax, though adamantly opposed to Hall's view, allowed that "Hall had considerable excuse, for many of the Eskimo stories, apparently about survivors of the lost expedition, were based upon actual occurrences." Nevertheless, he noted that "the Eskimos had little comprehension of time and number, and, furthermore, probably sometimes confused localities," which rendered their testimony, "even when related in apparent good faith by eye-witnesses ... extremely misleading if accepted as literally true." Unable to discount the tales of white men on the Melville Peninsula completely, Cyriax concluded that "reports, which Hall at first believed to concern survivors of the Franklin expedition, in fact related to members of other expeditions."[69] Cyriax concurred with the general opinion that "there can be no reasonable doubt that Rae was the man whom Kia saw, not during the autumn of 1854, as Koolooa and some other Eskimos seemed to imply, but in May 1847."[70] Yet the doubts remain, and they call for a more searching examination of the career and travels of Dr John Rae.

JOHN RAE

John Rae, the fourth son of John Rae and Margaret Glen Campbell of the Hall of Clestrain, was born on 30 September 1813. As a boy growing up in the windswept Orkney Islands north of Scotland, young John became accustomed to a rough life with few creature comforts. He thrived on physical challenges, remarking that "my chief and almost sole amusements during vacation or play hours were boating, shooting, fishing and riding (chiefly the three first)."[71] Rae described himself as "seasoned as to care little about cold or wet ... a moderately good climber among rocks, and not a bad walker."[72] His protracted journeys still stand as models of endurance, self-reliance, and efficiency.

Rae was as intelligent as he was hardy. He graduated in medicine from Edinburgh University in 1833 and was promptly en-

Dr John Rae at the height of his fame
(National Archives of Canada)

gaged by the Hudson's Bay Company, which had found that Orcadians were particularly suited to life in the wilds of Canada. Taking passage on the company ship *Prince of Wales*, Rae was sent to Moose Factory, where he served as a clerk and surgeon until 1844, when he was appointed to Rupert's River district.[73] The same year that Franklin set out from England, Rae was given a special commission by the Hudson's Bay Company's governor, George Simpson; he was to complete the survey of the Arctic coastline between Castor and Pollux River and Cape Englefield, points that had been reached by Dease and Simpson (1839) and Parry (1822), respectively. On his way north, while on the Winnipeg River, Rae encountered the fur trader Robert Ballantyne, who was greatly impressed by the young man:

In the afternoon we met another canoe, in which we saw a gentleman sitting ... the stranger introduced himself as Dr. Rae. He was on his way to York Factory, for the purpose of fitting out at that post an expedition for the survey of the small part of the North American coast left unexplored by Messrs. Dease and Simpson, which will then prove beyond a doubt whether or not there is a communication by water between the Atlantic and Pacific oceans round the north of America. He was very muscular and active, full of animal spirits, and had a fine intellectual countenance. He was considered, by those who knew him well, to be one of the best snow-shoe walkers in the service, was also an excellent rifle-shot, and could stand an immense amount of fatigue ... He does not proceed as other expeditions have done – namely, with large supplies of provisions and men, but merely takes a very small supply of provisions, and ten or twelve men ... He is of such a pushing, energetic character ... that there is every probability he will endeavour to prosecute his discoveries during winter, if at all practicable.[74]

Rae arrived at York Factory on 8 October 1845 and spent the winter there. Departing with ten men and two boats on 13 June 1846, he reached Fort Churchill on the twenty-seventh. After resting for a week, the expedition began in earnest, reaching Repulse Bay on 25 July. As if to prove Ballantyne's estimate of his "pushing, energetic character," Rae immediately set out across the narrow isthmus (now named after him) which separated, as the Inuit told him, Iwillik and Akkoolee (Repulse and Committee bays). The weather was foul and Rae, who was prevented from tracing the coastline in either direction by heavy ice, prudently returned to Repulse Bay to establish winter quarters. Unknown to Rae, just one month later the *Erebus* and *Terror* would become locked in their icy prison 300 miles to the west. At Repulse Bay, Rae and his men built a small and drafty stone hut, grandiloquently named Fort Hope, to shelter them over winter. Rae, who was the only non-smoker of the group, divided the structure into rooms by erecting a canvas partition to isolate himself from his men. True to his philosophy of "living off the land," the group spent the autumn hunting caribou and birds, and fishing in the nearby lakes.

On 5 April 1847 Rae once again set out across the isthmus and proceeded to trace the uncharted coast to the west. Two weeks later he arrived at the southeast corner of Lord Mayor's Bay, joining his discoveries with those of James Clark Ross, who had come from the north during an earlier expedition. Rae had thus demonstrated the truth of the native assertions that there were no outlets to the west in the southern reaches of the Gulf of Boothia and that Boothia was indeed a peninsula rather than an island. This had been in doubt since the expedition of Dease and Simpson in 1839, and the solution of this question had been the primary reason for the present survey. Nevertheless, the idea of this chimerical southern "passage" persisted:

During Rae's outward and return journeys he completely examined the whole of the west coast of Committee Bay, with the single exception of the south end of Pelly Bay. He did not actually walk round Pelly Bay, but distinctly saw land there from the summit, seven hundred and thirty feet above sea level, of Helen Island. Since he did not traverse this part of the bay, some geographers were unwilling to admit that the possible existence of a channel leading westwards from Pelly Bay had been finally disproved, but Rae himself was by now fully convinced that the land was continuous all round the south end of the bay.[75]

Arriving back at Fort Hope on 5 May, Rae again allowed himself only a week's rest before setting out. This time he proposed to tackle the short gap in the chart of the Arctic coastline between Committee Bay and the western end of Fury and Hecla Strait. It was during this journey northward along the western shore of the Melville Peninsula that Rae, as most historians have concluded, was seen by Kia.

THE MOST FATIGUING JOURNEY

On 13 May 1847 Rae left his base at Repulse Bay and again crossed the isthmus to Committee Bay. He took with him four "picked men" and the native Ouligbuck as "deer hunter and interpreter." A support party of three further men (one Inuit) carried provisions on a dogsled and accompanied the main group for three days. Once the exploring party had reached "Akkoolee," the supplies were transferred and the support team returned to Repulse Bay, accompanied by Ouligbuck, who "was unable to walk so fast as was desirable."[76] The four men who remained and accompanied Rae northward were a "Highlander" named Peter Matheson, a "Canadian" named Hilard Mineau, and two fellow Orcadians, John Folster and "our snow-house builder" John Corrigal.[77] The movements of these five men will to a large extent determine whether any of them could have been seen by Kia and Koolooa.

Rae had been told by the Inuit of Repulse Bay that the coast for which he was heading was very difficult to travel on and that they themselves never journeyed that way. Nor could Rae persuade them to do so. Despite the promise of a "much coveted gun" to any Inuit guide, none of the Inuit volunteered, for "they said it was impossible to travel with sledges" that way. "They were quite willing enough to go by Ig-loo-lik," noted Rae, "but of course this would have been of no use, and I could not explore the unknown coast by that route."[78] So Rae and his four companions set out alone. "Each of the party was laden with 60 or 70 Lbs," recorded Rae. "My own load was only about 40 Lbs. but as I led the way this trifling weight was quite enough."[79]

The journey proved to be "the most fatiguing" of Rae's career, and he remarked that "although not very stout when I set out, I had to tighten my belt six inches before my return."[80] The coast trended almost due north once the Rae isthmus had been crossed, and at first progress was rapid. Rae noticed a large island offshore in the depths of Committee Bay, which the natives had told him was called "Shatook" and which he named Prince of Wales (now shortened to Wales) Island. This island was a famed repository of wood – the Inuit told Rae that "large trees grew" there. Hall later heard the same thing and concluded that "the Innuits truly think so, but from some erroneous cause."[81]

By 22 May, Rae's party had arrived at Fraser Bay. Here Rae and Corrigal went hunting caribou.[82] Although Fraser Bay is sixty miles to the south of Kia and Koolooa's hunting area, this is the only time that Rae specifically mentions hunting during his journey. This prompted Cyriax to conclude that it was here that Koolooa heard the gunshots.[83] After Fraser Bay, nothing important occurred until the party approached Garry Bay, which was known to the Inuit as Arlangnazhu. This was the area where Kia and Koolooa's six companions later prosecuted their hunt, and it was also where Kia's sister would come across the strange footprints.

On 25 May the group built a snow house. According to Rae, this was "in Latitude 68°–48' north, Longde. 85°–4' w. near a small stream frozen (– like all others we had passed –) to the bottom."[84] Here the party divided. Two men (Folster and Mineau) were left behind "to fish and shoot" while the other three carried on north, crossing Garry Bay and establishing a campsite at Cape Miles. Rae determined his position here by "a good meridian observation of the sun"[85] (which was quite accurate), and here the party again divided. Rae's *Narrative of an Expedition* tells of the next day, the pivotal one for our purposes:

Our provisions being now nearly all used, I could advance only half a night's journey further to the northward, and return the following morning to our present quarters. Leaving one of the men, I set out with the other at half-past 9 P.M., the snow falling fast; and although we had little or nothing to carry, the travelling was very fatiguing as we crossed Baker Bay – so named in memory of a much valued friend – at the north side of which we arrived after a walk of four miles. It now snowed so thick that we could not see farther than fifty yards around us, and we were consequently obliged to follow the windings of the shore, which, when we had traced it six miles beyond Baker Bay, turned sharp to the eastward; but the weather continuing thick, I could not see how far it preserved this trending.

After waiting here nearly an hour, the sky cleared up for a few minutes at 4 A.M., which enabled me to discover that we were on the south shore of a considerable bay, and I could also obtain a distinct view of the coast line for nearly twelve miles beyond it.

To the most distant visible point (latitude 69°42′ N, longitude 85°8′ W) I gave the name of Cape Ellice, after Edward Ellice, Esq. M.P., one of the Directors of the Company; the bay to the northward, and the headland on which we stood, were respectively named after the distinguished navigators Sir Edward Parry and Captain Crozier.

Finding it hopeless to attempt reaching the strait of the Fury and Hecla, from which Cape Ellice could not be more than ten miles distant, we took possession of our discoveries with the usual formalities, and retraced our steps, arriving at our encampment of the previous day at half-past 8 A.M.[86]

The man Rae had left at Cape Miles had had a trying night:

We found that Matheson, the man left behind, had built a snowhouse after a fashion of his own, the walls being like those of a stone building, and the roof covered in the same way with slabs of snow placed on the opposite walls in a slanting position, so as to rest on one another in the centre. Seven hours had been spent in building this edifice, which was not a very handsome one; but being sufficiently wide, and, when our legs were doubled up a little, long enough for us all when lying down, we found it pretty comfortable.[87]

It is not impossible that some Inuit later came across Matheson's unusual dwelling, built on the pattern of a stone building and certainly "not such as Innuits ever make," and that the story of it was garbled in transmission to Hall.

Rae, Corrigal, and Matheson promptly set out to rejoin their two companions who had been left encamped to the south of Garry Bay. The two groups had been separated for five days, and Rae found Folster and Mineau "well, but very *thin*, as they had neither caught nor shot anything eatable except two marmots – had we been absent twelve hours more, they were to have cooked a piece of parchment skin for supper."[88] Despite the foul weather and poor hunting, Rae and his men then "marched merrily on," as he recorded, "tightening our belts (mine came in six inches) the men vowing that when they got on full allowance, they would make up for lost time."[89] They arrived back at Fort Hope on 9 June 1847. They had seen no signs of any Inuit on the west coast and were completely unaware that they had been observed on their march.

RAE VERSUS HALL

Rae's short journey of May 1847 was useful in a cartographical sense, but when placed against his subsequent achievements it is hardly worthy of much note. For thirty-two years there was little need to remark on it, but in 1879 Professor Nourse completed his editing of the fragmentary notes left behind by the now-deceased Hall, and Kia's story of a stranger came to light. By 1881 Rae had heard of the story and read the book, and he asserted that he must have been the stranger seen by Kia.

Before analysing the evidence, some mention must be made of the complex personalities involved. After hearing the tales of Inuit encounters with strangers, Hall believed beyond a shadow of a doubt that the Melville Peninsula stories dealt with Franklin's men. Nowhere in his writings or later letters did Hall ever cast doubt on the veracity of his Igloolik informants. Even after returning from the Arctic, disillusioned by his lack of success, he was unshakeably convinced that some unexplained events had transpired in that remote corner of the Arctic.

Hall's editor, Nourse, at pains to treat his subject fairly, could not fail to see that Hall was prone to accept Inuit testimony literally, especially when it corroborated Hall's preconceived ideas of what had befallen the lost men of the Franklin expedition. Nourse kindly attributed this to Hall's being a "singleminded trusting man, who believed that others were like himself."[90] Cyriax's judgment was harsher. According to him, Hall was ill-suited in some respects for his vocation: "The fundamental causes of [Hall's] initial mistake are not far to seek. According to those who knew him, he lacked general knowledge ... His enthusiasm, courage, and perseverance are beyond dispute, but he was unquestionably far too ready to accept as strictly true any Eskimo information that served to confirm his preconceived ideas, and he cannot be said to have approached the subject with an entirely open mind."[91] Moreover, Hall was a stubborn and opinionated man. According to his biographer, he was "not a man to meddle with; aroused, he was capable of intemperate words and, as his later career showed, intemperate action ... Hall often seemed to enjoy combat for combat's sake."[92] He was constantly suspicious of his Inuit companions, often remarking that he expected a sudden attempt on his life, and at one point he shot and killed a hired whaler whom he charged with mutinous intentions.

The other prime character in the Kia stories was also unconventional. Rae, after years of arduous and noteworthy work in the Arctic and the Canadian wilderness, had by 1881 retired to London, England. He was still a fit and handsome fellow. Twelve years later, his obituary notice remarked that "although born ... eighty years ago, until his last illness, no more vigorous looking or active man walked the streets of London."[93] Yet although well respected by the public at large, Rae felt with some reason that he had not been given the credit and rewards that his exemplary service deserved.

It will be remembered that in 1847 Rae had asserted (correctly) that there was no outlet to the west in the southern reaches of the Gulf of Boothia and that Boothia itself was a peninsula, as the Inuit had told the Ross expedition in 1830. This was extremely unwelcome news to Sir William Barrow, secretary of the Admiralty and self-proclaimed Arctic expert, who only the year before had published a book which claimed that a passage would be found in that precise place. Barrow and his coterie of naval officers pointed out that Rae had not actually traversed the entire coastline around Pelly Bay and that he had had only a vague view of the southern reaches from the heights of Helen Island. Undoubtedly prompted not a little by disdain for a "fur trapper," these men refused to accept Rae's word without proof. Rae returned to the Arctic in 1854 and completed the survey, making a point of walking over the disputed ground.

Rae's contributions to geography and science were barely acknowledged in official circles. Among the relics left to the Edinburgh museum on his death was his Arctic medal. Tellingly, it was fitted with "five clasps, not apparently official," denoting Rae's personal accomplishments and presumably made at his own request.[94] One biographer wondered if Rae's "openly expressed attitude to the Navy stood in the way of his being recommended to the Queen for a Knighthood which his reputation and his achievements as an explorer would have amply justified?"[95] Never a great admirer of the naval exploratory method which, in his opinion, used large and expensive ships and crews to accomplish less than he and his few men could do while living off the land, Rae grew increasingly embittered. Known as "no enthusiast for the Admiralty nor for the naval explorers,"[96] the hardy Orcadian, more comfortable in a canoe or tent than in the boardrooms of fashionable London society, soon realized that he would never be truly accepted by the predominantly naval circle of contemporary Arctic explorers.

Rae's personality did not help. As revealed in his logs and letters, he was a stern and serious man, rarely given to humour and not noticeably modest. He could not brook any implied criticism, and he had a temper that was "quick and somewhat fiery."[97] Twenty years after Rae's death, the famed Arctic explorer Vilhjalmur Stefansson gave a speech at the Royal Geographical Society in which he noted that Rae remained "a controversial figure":

When I launched upon a eulogy of Rae I sensed a division among [the audience], and during the rest of my talk I felt as if points which I made that could be construed as favourable to Rae met the approval of some and the disapproval of others ... Sir Ernest Shackleton told me at the close, that "a few old fogies" took the position that "anybody can succeed, *if* he is willing to go native." Rae was apparently considered in certain quarters as not having been quite in the high tradition of the gentleman explorer.[98]

Stefansson also noted that "it was evidently a weakness of Rae's to be ungenerous to the weaknesses of others."[99] Even the most admiring biographer could not ignore the less flattering aspects of Rae's character:

Kindly and generous though he was to those who worked with him and for him, he had no hesitation in fighting for credit where credit was due. There were sharp passages with Sir Clements Markham, the Secretary of the Royal Geographical Society, who seemed to ignore the explorations of Hudson's Bay Company men. From Rae's viewpoint, Markham belonged to a Navy clique, with whose methods of Arctic travel Rae frequently took issue. Then, too the Hydrographer for the Admiralty, Captain Washington, in a chart of Collinson's travels in Wollaston and Victoria Lands, wrote an attached note giving credit to Collinson for part of the mapping which had previously been done by Simpson and by Rae. Rae, after a stormy passage at arms, made Washington withdraw the note, but made him an enemy for life. [100]

His own explorations ignored, Rae was chagrined to find that his greatest claim to fame lay in the information he brought back to England about the worst naval disaster in exploration history. And he was to find that even this achievement was tainted.

The first stories Rae heard of "very many dead white men" were "too vague to act upon," and although he unknowingly approached within a few miles of the disaster site, he did not learn this until months later when he interviewed the natives at Repulse Bay. He then returned to England with his news, only to find himself again the object of controversy. The Admiralty had offered a sizable reward to anyone bringing information concerning Franklin's men, and it was whispered that Rae had raced home for the money rather than staying in the Arctic and pursuing the leads given by the Inuit. Rae professed his innocence; he had spent most of the past decade in Canada, and he claimed, undoubtedly with justification, that he had had no knowledge of the reward. Yet even Franklin's widow Jane, fearful that payment of the reward would signal the government's withdrawal from the search for her husband and thus the resolution of his fate, publicly campaigned to belittle Rae's efforts.

Rae, the eternal outsider, was also vilified in the press for revealing the details about cannibalism which the Inuit had told him.

This, too, was patently unfair, since Rae had offered to suppress this aspect of his report and had been told by the Admiralty that this would not be necessary. Also, having predicted that the navy would meet disaster in forcing large ships through ice-choked channels, Rae was not honoured for bringing proof that he had been right.

However justified Rae's combative attitude may have been, it complicates the issue when trying to determine whether he was the man seen on Melville Peninsula. While he was disdainful and resentful of the naval officers who had slighted him, he was ruthless in his criticism of Hall, the American iconoclast who, more than any other, adopted Rae's own method of living with the native people and travelling light. In two scathing letters, Rae developed a theme of invidious comparison and overwhelming sarcasm which, when read today, make one wince at the view of a great man's petty jealousies.

Remarking on Hall's (or, rather, Nourse's) book, Rae felt duty bound to point out the "careless manner of writing and apparent indifference to the facts."[101] As for Kia's account, he found it "a story which bears on the face of it strong evidence of error and falsehood."[102] Rae's detailed critique of the work, especially in any place where his own travels or opinions were mentioned, belied his claim to have given it only a cursory inspection. Much of his criticism was irrelevant, as when he pointed out Hall's error in finding only two small lakes where Rae himself had previously found three (even though Rae admitted that one of the lakes was so small as to be a "pond"). Rae further complained at great length about the maps included in Nourse's edition, which were drawn after Hall's death and over which Hall consequently had no editorial control. Rae noted that "my name is left out on about six hundred miles of my discoveries ... Hall's name being substituted ... at which I am not much surprised ... One effect of this chart is to give credit to Hall for surveys that had been made by others years before."[103] In fact, Hall had been impressed with Rae's achievements, specifically remarking in his notes that "Rae's chart [is] to be relied on"[104] and "the chart of Dr Rae's very good – I have had great assistance from it ... I am surprised to find such precision in the Geographic work wh. Dr Rae has performed in this country."[105]

Having been slighted by others, Rae was most reluctant to allow

Hall any credit for his own work. In a recurring theme, Rae complained that "great credit is taken to himself by Hall, and also given to him by Nourse ... for completing the survey of the west shore of Melville Peninsula, only eight miles of which I did not see in 1847." From Rae's original narrative, the one made at the time, this eight-mile gap was the result of lack of provisions, but by 1877 he was attributing it to "a defect in the only map I had with me."[106] In any case, Rae's estimate of the gap is disingenuous; he probably knew in 1847 – and he must have known thirty years later – that the gap was nearer twenty miles than the eight of his field estimate.

Rae drew unflattering comparisons between Hall's long sojourn in the Arctic and his own two visits to Repulse Bay, noting that Hall was supported by the nearby whalers (who, in fact, were often a hindrance to his work) and even going so far as to imply that Hall lived a luxurious life among the Inuit, warmly ensconced in their igloos, while Rae himself had to sleep in cold cheerless isolation:

Our sledge work was much more arduous than Hall's, because he had large teams of dogs, while we did our own hauling, and for nearly five hundred miles on one occasion carried everything on our backs, the ice and coast being too rough for sledging, a feat never even attempted before in Arctic service, nor easily done, except by men accustomed to carry loads of 100 pounds over rough ground, as we were. The journeys of this spring (1847) with sledges exceeded 1,200 miles on one of my Arctic sledge journeys, with only two pretty smart men. We travelled 1,100 miles at the good average of twenty five miles a day, every step of which we walked, and either hauling a sledge or carrying a moderate load all the way ...

My spring sledge work of 1874 [sic – 1847] will bear fair comparison with his two chief sledge journeys, and that portion by which I examined the west coast of Melville peninsula to within eight miles of Fury and Hecla Strait by carrying everything on our backs – sledging being impracticable – could not have been done by him (Hall) with his native assistants. This was shown by the very roundabout and lengthy journey he took to reach and return from the west entrance of the Fury and Hecla Strait, adding about three-fifths to the distance travelled over.[107]

This last observation is representative of the irrelevancies in Rae's diatribe. Hall was not interested in exploring unknown coast; his aim was to locate the Inuit, and quite naturally he took the easier, if roundabout, traditional route. Direct comparisons of the daily distance travelled by Rae and Hall are also simplistic. Hall, at the mercy of his guides, was often delayed while the Inuit went afield in pursuit of game, so he could not force the same pace as a disciplined exploring party. He often bemoaned this fact in his notebooks and asserted that he would never be placed in that position again.

Not content with ridiculing Hall's methods (so similar to his own), Rae then shifts his target to cast aspersions on Tookoolitoo, Hall's interpreter.

Hall readily believes all the "traditions" about Franklin's party and a supposed Crozier, whenever they tend to promote his own peculiar views, of which he gave us some insight before he went on this expedition, and it sometimes looks as if his very able interpreter lent her aid in constructing these so-called "traditions" ... My interpreter both in 1847 and 1854 was an excellent one, but he had not sufficient knowledge of the subject to "coach" the Esquimaux what to say, nor had I at the time, so we could not do so, even had I been inclined, which is not likely.[108]

This line of attack was totally unworthy. Tookoolitoo (and to a lesser extent her husband Ebierbing) was the ideal helpmate for any white man wishing to gather Inuit testimony. She was observant and intelligent, and having lived for a time in both England and the United States, she was comfortable in both cultures. When Hall first met Tookoolitoo, she was dressed in "crinoline, heavy flounces, an attenuated toga, and an immensely expanded 'kiss-me quick' bonnet." As he later recalled, "She spoke my own language fluently, and there, seated in the main cabin, I had a long and interesting conversation with her."[109] A few days later, Hall visited Tookoolitoo at home in her igloo, where she served him tea and complained about the whalers' propensity for profanity.[110] Even Cyriax, who agreed with Rae's conclusions, could not support this attack on Hall's friends: "Both Joe [Ebierbing] and Hannah [Tookoolitoo] were most faithful servants, and there is no reason to suspect that either of them would ever have purposely altered any of the Eskimo stories. Hannah was Hall's usual interpreter; she had no real difficulties with local Eskimo dialects, and spoke English fluently."[111]

Despite his unsavoury personal attacks on Hall and his complaints against him, Rae's contention that he himself was the man seen by Kia has been almost universally accepted. Since no other explorer is known to have approached the spot during the relevant period, this has been taken as an "open and shut case," Rae getting the nod by default. But beyond the fact that he had travelled along the relevant coastline, Rae offered little evidence that he had inspired Kia's story. He noted that "the description of the coat with a hood, worn by the white man said to have been seen near Cape Crozier, was exactly that used by me in 1847 when there – a 'capot,' almost universally worn by all Hudson Bay Company's people in winter."[112] But to the Inuit, all white men's clothing was similar and could hardly be used to identify individuals.

Rae was on firmer ground when attacking Hall's dating of Kia's sighting. Rae found that "this fitting in of dates" was "rather wonderful": "When I revisited Repulse Bay in 1854, all my old friends there told me that I had been absent only five years, whereas seven winters had elapsed. Yet Hall gets these very Esquimaux to trace back accurately for thirteen years!"[113] Rae correctly noted that "the great difficulty with the Esquimaux is to obtain correct dates and numbers – I have seen an Esquimaux and his wife completely puzzled to tell how many children they had, the total number being only four or five – none of the natives could tell me how many years had elapsed since I had been with them before."[114]

The Inuit difficulty with and disinterest in exact dating has been well documented, but it should be noted that stating the number of children in a family could be a complicated matter. Inuit "families" were very fluid, freely including adoptions, occasional polygamy and polyandry, and temporary "marriages." Moreover, Hall's Inuit acquaintances specifically told him that Rae had visited Repulse Bay twice, exactly seven years apart.[115]

Although the Inuit who heard his story unfailingly asserted that Kia's stranger had been a kobluna (white man), Kia had originally identified him as an Etkerlin (Indian). Rae seized on this fact as verification that he had inspired the story.

It is as certain as anything can be that no American Indians ever visited that part of the Arctic lands, except the two Indian hunters (Nibitabo and Mistegan) that accompanied me. I had with me in 1847 and also in 1854 several half breeds – as fine fellows as ever a commander could wish to have with him – who had dark complexions, and who were supposed by the Esquimaux to be Indians … No Indians except those with me in 1847 and 1854 and my halfbreeds (who were believed by the Esquimaux to be Indians) had within the last half century, if ever, visited Melville Peninsula. The Indians have a most wholesome dread of the Innuit, unless they can pounce upon a small and weak party on the borders of their own hunting grounds.[116]

The "Indian question" is also largely irrelevant. Kia's stranger, whose face was "white, not dark," was undoubtedly a white man. In any case, none of Rae's Indian or half-breed companions accompanied him to the Melville Peninsula. In addition, Rae's assertion that "no Indians … had within the last half century, if ever, visited Melville Peninsula" is demonstrably false. Although contact between the Inuit and the Indians of Hudson Bay was rare, it was not impossible. Hall was told that "Indians certainly do make their way sometimes up as far North as the neighbourhood of Neitch-il-le. Some of the Neitch-il-lee Innuits have had many severe fights with them. So Ou-e-la & his brothers have told me … There is one Indian living with the Neitch-il-lee Innuits. He has a family & the Innuits there are very fond of him."[117]

While wintering his ships at Winter Island (1821–22), William Parry had found that the natives, none of whom had actually seen an Indian, "seemed well acquainted" with their "ferocity and decided hostility to their own nation." Parry also learned that the Inuit were aware that Indians paddled strange canoes and made use of snowshoes similar in design to that used by the white men.[118] At Igloolik, Parry noted that "of the Indians they know enough by tradition to hold them in considerable dread, on account of their cruel and ferocious manners."[119]

In truth, Rae's evidence that he was the subject of Kia's story is rather flimsy, being based on little more than proximity and clothing. In addition, there are several conflicting details between the accounts given by the Inuit hunters and that preserved in Rae's writings. Are both parties talking of the same incident?

DISCREPANCIES

The first question to be asked is geographical – where exactly did Kia see the stranger? The answer seems straightforward: "the place was near the N.W. extreme of Melville Peninsula as he (Koo-loo) points out on Parry's Chart."[120] Kia told his listeners that the place where he saw the stranger was "very near the sea-ice."[121] He further and rather unhelpfully defined the location by noting that it was "not far from Ar-lang-na-zhoo (Garry Bay)."[122] He more specifically remarked that the place was "by the w. extreme of Fury & Hecla Strait not far from a river which runs into the sea from the eastward."[123]

Other Inuit corroborated this: "The place where Ki-a saw the stranger is not a great ways below Adge-go (Fury & Hecla St) near the great sea and w. side of the big land & the stranger going toward the long point near where a river is."[124] Koolooa's account of the Inuit movements confirms that the sightings occurred near the northwest corner of Melville Peninsula, for after seeing the stranger and the strange tracks, he and Kia moved south and rejoined their hunting companions who had been searching for game near Arlangnazhu (Garry Bay).

But how trustworthy is a general description such as "the extreme point?" Luckily, Koolooa served as Hall's guide on a trip to the west coast, and he pointed out the exact place. Hall stated that when proceeding to Parry Bay from Encampment Bay, while west of Cape Ellice, Koolooa pointed "to southward saying there is the land where Ki-a saw that man."[125] He later confirmed that "Ki-a saw the stranger down on the land by this our 7th enct."[126] Hall's seventh encampment, as clearly shown on his track chart, was to the north of Parry Bay. Not only was this to the north, miles beyond Rae's farthest point of travel, but "the Et-ker-lin as Ki-a supposed the man to be [was] passing to the North."[127]

Koolooa also pointed out the exact place where he himself had seen the stranger's tracks and heard the gunshot. This was inland, west of Grinnell Lake, near the Brevoort River. Again, Hall had camped at the place, noting that his party stopped "for making our 5th Igloo since leaving Oo-glit close by the place where the tracks were seen & the gun report by Koo-loo-a."[128] Hall's fifth encampment, of 20 April 1868, is shown clearly on his track chart, and his listing (no. 148) gives the position as 69°42'N, 85°00'w.[129] Again, this seems definitive, as does Hall's note that "Koo-loo-a saw the strange tracks where we had our 5th Igloo & 2 days after this Ki-a saw the stranger down on the land by this our 7th enct."[130] None of these facts are compatible with a meet-

ing with Rae or Corrigal, neither of whom travelled this far north
or left the coast.

Hall also obliquely mentions that "White men's tracks were
seen" even farther inland, "near the head of Quilliam Creek,"[131]
but as this is near the site of Parry's operations in the 1820s, these
reported tracks are less definitive. Interestingly, the Inuit were certain that someone had been hunting in the area.

Nut-er-lik has told me today through "Jo" as interpreter that some of the
Innuits about here have hunted from time to time Polar Bears up toward
Adge-go & that they have often wondered why it was that the Bears appeared very shy running away at once on seeing the Innuits. Not many
years ago finally a Bear killed & it had a fresh wound as of a lance or something like it. Much wonderment about this matter as well as about the general shyness of the Bears toward Adge-go. Innuits have thought that it
might be a certain Innuit or Innuits of Too-noo-nee-noo-shuk [Ponds Bay]
that killed some other Innuits & ran away might be living near Ar-lang-
na-zhoo or between there and Adge-go.[132]

The second discrepancy is with timing. Temporarily leaving
aside the question of the year of the encounter, we note that Kia saw
his stranger walking in the morning and that Koolooa had declined
to accompany him, since he wanted to clean the caribou he had
killed the day before. Rae and Corrigal left Cape Miles at 9 P.M., arrived at Cape Crozier at 3 A.M., and were back at Cape Miles by
8 A.M. the next morning.

Even more convincing than the discrepancy in the time of day is
that of season. While the Inuit may have had trouble determining
exact dates, they were far more attuned to the variations of the
short seasons in their land than the white men were. And they uniformly stated that Kia saw his stranger "in the summer of the year
– when took-too had short hair – no snow on the ground."[133] The
lack of snow was a consistent feature: "the tracks were in the sand
for it was in the fall when snow was off the ground."[134] Koolooa
was amazed by the strange footprints, so fresh that the trodden
grass was still recovering.

Rae's journey took place between 13 May and 9 June 1847 (the
relevant part being 27–8 May), which, although arguably "summer" in temperate climes, is still well in advance of the short Arctic
summer. Rae was quite graphic in his description of the weather

conditions as he and Corrigal made their quick excursion north from Cape Miles. He noted that "the snow falling fast ... it snowed so thick that we could not see farther than fifty yards around us," and on arrival at Cape Crozier he found "the weather continuing thick"; Rae had to wait an hour until "the sky cleared up for a few minutes at 4 A.M."[135] But Kia had made no mention of a thick snowstorm or of reduced visibility in his detailed description of his progress from rock to rock as he kept the stranger in sight at all times.

Then again, Kia and Koolooa were alerted to the presence of the strangers by hearing the reports of their guns. Yet in none of Rae's accounts (his published *Narrative*, the official report to the Hudson's Bay Company, or his letters) is there any indication that he and Corrigal did any hunting or fired their weapons at all when they were in the appropriate area. Matheson, who had been left behind at Cape Miles, was entirely occupied in building his makeshift igloo during their absence, and even Folster and Mineau, far to the south in Garry Bay, "had neither caught nor shot anything eatable except two marmots."[136]

The discrepancies mount: Kia saw only one man, whereas Rae never mentions having separated from Corrigal; after seeing the stranger, Kia and Koolooa came across the tracks of a party of three men and a dog, whereas Rae had only the one companion and "as the dogs were of little use during the last journey, I took none with me."[137] Yet these problems were all set aside by the historians. Kia must have seen Rae because there was no one else available.

What was needed was one piece of physical evidence that would make the testimonial differences irrelevant. And one was found.

THE MONUMENT

Kia and Koolooa had undoubtedly seen a strange white man and the footprints of a party, and had heard shots fired while hunting. Their testimony was clear and consistent, and even without any physical evidence to support it, it was corroborated by the testimony of Kudloon and others to such an extent that there can be no reasonable suspicion of falsehood. But there was also some physical evidence. Hall was shown at least one thing that was probably the handiwork of white men: the day after Kia saw his stranger, the "same day" the two of them came across the tracks of three white men and a dog, Koolooa found a curious monument.[138] He later described this discovery to Hall:

After the death of Ki-a, Koo-loo-a thought he would go deer hunting in that part of the country where Ki-a had seen the strange person, as he believed he might find something that would be useful to him there-abouts and as he wanted some wood with which he might make arrows & spear heandles [sic] between Ar-lang-naz-u & the NW Cape of Melville Peninsula. He hunted but found nothing that he sought for. Here I asked if he (Koo-loo-a) during his search found any piles of stone called In-nook-shoo, by the natives. He replied that he did. I then got Rae's chart & placed it before us. Koo-loo-a soon comprehended its nature & then said that the extreme NW part of the Melville Penn & sea by it of the chart was not as the land & water really are. He said that quite a large river runs from the eastward nearly parrelel [sic] with Adge-go (Fury & Hecla Straight [sic]) & empties its waters into a Bay very near to Cape Ellice of Rae's discovery in 1847. Near the river south side of it Koo-loo-a found a monument of stone on the crest of a piece of rising ground & a little to one side west of the monument he found where a curious kind of *cache* had been made of stones. The cache had been opened & the stone all thrown on one side. The monument & the *cache* stones all shewed a great degree of freshness. He did not think they were the work of any Innuit. He looked carefully about where the cache had been made for the object to learn what had been deposited there. No signs that any meat had ever been put there. He does not think that any Innuit had ever before been so high up from Ar-lang-na-zhu (Garry Bay of Rae's chart).[139]

Koolooa believed that the cairn and cache were associated with Kia's stranger, and his description so interested Hall that he determined to visit the site. Koolooa gladly offered to act as guide, and with Tookoolitoo and Ebierbing as interpreters, Hall's small party set off for the western shore in late April 1868.

On the twentieth, as previously mentioned, Hall's party camped on Brevoort River near the place where the tracks of white men had been seen.[140] Hall's editor Nourse considered the events of the following few days significant enough to render Hall's field notes verbatim:

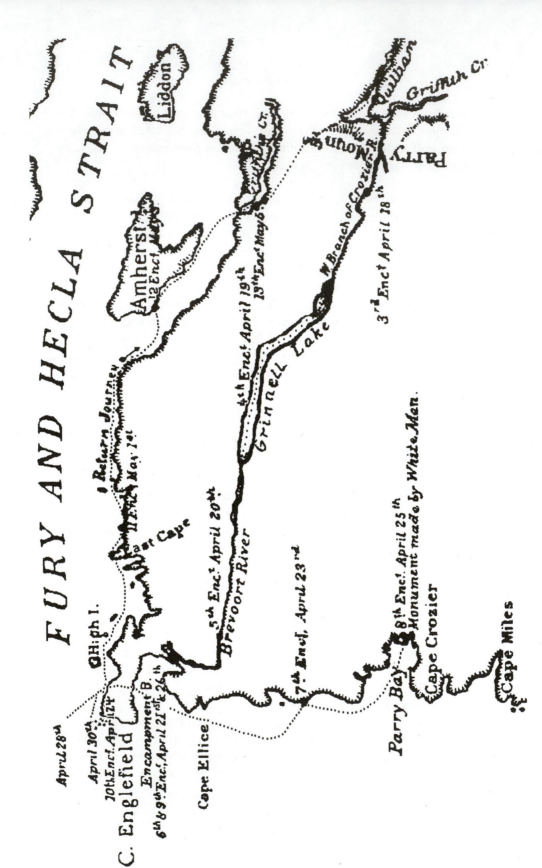

Hall's track chart, showing his route to the monument (Smithsonian Institution)

The monument at Parry Bay (Smithsonian Institution)

Literal copy of Hall's notes: "APRIL 24. – Koo-loo-a requested today that I would take a look with my spy-glass in a certain direction, after we had tramped for four hours over hill, lake, ravine, and through deep snow. I looked, and sighted a monument above the snow. Koo-loo-a and Frank [Lailor] took a look through the spy-glass, the former declaring that the monument he saw was at the head of a bay not then in sight … To-morrow morning, I remove with my party to the monument. Koo-loo-a told Hannah [Tookoolitoo] that when he first saw this monument thirteen years before, it was then fresh, and now looks old. When he found it and the cache-stones under the bank, he told all the Innuits of his strange discovery. No Inuit could have made it. A hole was dug out of the rocks and something deposited in it. Afterward, the stones covering the cache were thrown all in a pile on one side, and the deposit, whatever it was, taken out …"[141]

The next day the party moved down to the site of the monument itself. Hall gave a detailed description of its setting: "On either side of the plain on which it stands is a river, and hills of delta are northeast of it. It is 100 feet above the sea, and near a hill upon the south side of the plain. The hill looks not unlike an inverted whale-boat when seen at a little distance from the northwest."[142] The site of Koolooa's cache was found to be "buried deep in a huge bank of snow that lies over the steep bank of ground running alongside of the plain on the margin of wh. is the monument."[143] Hall's field notes describe his investigation of it:

APRIL 25. – This morning we leave our seventh *igloo* here and move down to the monument, to make all investigations possible relating to it, and try our best to find the cache …

8 a.m. – Passing along frem [*sic*] seventh encampment toward Cape Crozier, the monument is distinctly visible with the glass. I and Frank commenced at once with our snow-shovels to cut out snow-blocks from the heavy bank just west of the monument in search of the cache-stones. *Koo-loo-a*, from his remembrance of the situation of the monument and cache-stones, has shown us where to dig.

10.5 a.m. – Hannah has found the tenting-place of white men – an ob-long tent and four fresh upturned stones, one at each corner, to make fast the lines of the tent; the stones show an age since turned up out of their bed the same as the monument stones.

10.30. – Joe, in searching around, has found *another* tenting-place. Frank and myself were busy raising blocks when Joe called, and then we all ran where he was, and have just made our investigations. *These* stones are in a circular form, and evidently the tenting-place of Innuits within ten to fifteen years. Hannah said if a fire-place could be found within the tent-circle then they were Innuit tenting places, and at last a fire-place was found within one of the circles – black on the back of the fire-place; a stone that had formed one side was loosened and turned up by Hannah and found black with smoke. *Koo-loo-a* found a large stone in proper po-sition for holding the line keeping up the entrance to the tent; as Ig-loo-lik people make their tents. Joe, Hannah, and *Koo-loo-a* are sure the *ob-long-shaped* tenting-place and the stones at the corners and outside row of small stones tell the truth, that Innuits never did that work. The contrast particularly striking between the tenting-place of the whites and that of the natives … All day we have been hard at work cutting out snow-blocks in search of the cache-stones, but in vain. One would be greatly de-lighted to see the excavations and upturned blocks all around made in searching for lost cache stones.[144]

The contrast between this tenting place and the circular one of Inuit design was overwhelming.[145] But Hall could not continue his efforts to find the cache, for the party's food was running perilous-ly short and it was time to return. Koo-loo-a "was the most disap-pointed one of the party, for he expressed honest fears that he would be thought to have told a falsehood. Yet his character for en-tire truthfulness had been and still remained unquestioned … He left the spot with the assurance that his search for the evidence of white men's having lived a struggling life in those regions had not been in vain, for they had found a monument and tenting-place made by WHITE MEN."[146] Before they left, Hall performed one more task. Aware that many Arctic explorers buried their records near or under conspicuous monuments, he dismantled the cairn, noting that "there was evidence enough that the ground about & under the monument had never been disturbed." Koolooa remarked that when he had found the monument, the stones had been as fresh "as if made the year before," but "now they look old."[147]

Who made the camp and built the cairn? If the unvarying testimony and the physical evidence is to be believed, both must have been constructed by white men. Koolooa had said he found the monument thirteen years before Hall's visit (that is, in 1854), and that the cairn was then remarkably fresh. Most historians believe that in 1854 it was in fact seven years old, for Hall's single best piece of evidence, the monument, was also claimed by Rae as his own.

Rae does not specifically state, either in his published *Narrative* or in his official report, that he built a cairn at the terminal point of his 1847 explorations. In his *Narrative* he noted only, "We took possession of our discoveries with the usual formalities."[148] We cannot know whether the "usual formalities" consisted of simply claiming the land for his sovereign or whether they involved erecting a lasting monument. Considering that Rae had but one assistant, that they had travelled over forty miles in rough conditions (with a one-hour stop), and that they nevertheless arrived back at camp within eleven hours, any cairn they may have built must have been a rough and ready structure indeed. Yet although Rae never mentioned it in any of his writings of 1847, in his 1881 letter he asserted that Hall's "monument" had most certainly been built by himself.

I had a cairn built there (according to my usual practice when stones could be found), not on the extreme point of the cape, but some miles east of it, and a note deposited therein recording briefly the work done. On my return to Repulse bay in 1853, the natives told me of this cairn, not knowing that it had been built by my men, and that three or four strangers (white men), or their footmarks, had been observed at the place or near it. I, of course, explained to them what I had done on a former visit seven years before. They (the natives) believed I had been only five years absent, and thought no more on the subject.[149]

Rae noted that "it is not the first time in arctic history that so small a mole-hill as the story of a cairn of stone and a few footsteps in the snow, has by lapse of time and frequent repetition grown into a very considerable mountain,"[150] and he even went so far as to imply that Hall knew that the monument was Rae's work! Rae found the fact that Hall, having spent so much effort in reaching the monument, stated that he could not find the cache because of the deep snow, "which should have easily been removed sufficiently for that purpose in half an hour," was "surprising beyond measure." He concluded that Hall must have excavated the site, uncovered Rae's record, "and for several reasons he may have thought it advisable not to make known the fact. It is with reluctance and regret," added Rae, "that I have come to this conclusion, because I can in no other way solve the difficulty."[151]

This accusation, as Rae must have known from his reading of Nourse's book, was unworthy and unjustified. Hall and his companions had found that Koolooa's "Innookshoo" had already been disturbed, so if Rae's record had been deposited there, it had undoubtedly been removed by the original discoverer, and there would have been no need for Hall to conceal its presence. In fact, if Rae had paid more attention to Hall's account, he would have noted that it was not the cairn but the "cache" that was covered in frozen snow. Moreover, Hall did not labour for a mere "half an hour" in his efforts to uncover it; he spent two days in the attempt. Nevertheless, if the cairn found by Koolooa was indeed built by Rae this, seemingly, should resolve the case. Koolooa's "Innookshoo" is inextricably tied in with the stranger seen by Kia, and Rae's claim to have been this man is substantially strengthened if the cairn was his. Unfortunately, as with many other elements of the case, things are not quite that clear.

As previously noted, in all Rae's accounts that were written at the time, Rae clearly indicated that he and Corrigal never entered Parry Bay (now named, curiously enough, Franklin Bay) but that they stopped "on the south shore of a considerable Bay" and that "the land where we stood was called Cape Crozier." The eminent scholar Cyriax noted that "Hall had Rae's track-chart with him. This showed that in May 1847 Rae had travelled … as far as Cape Cro-

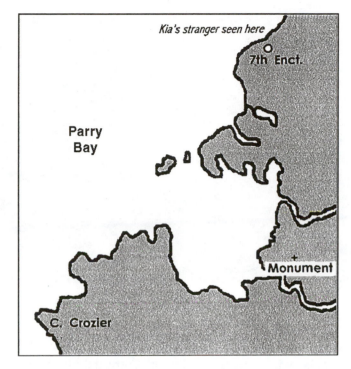

"Monumental Inlet," as drawn by Hall (Smithsonian Institution)

zier, on the south side of Parry Bay, but had retraced his steps before reaching the site of the cairn."[152] While Cyriax was not ready to accept Hall's hypothesis that the cairn and cache had been made by Franklin survivors, as an honest scholar he had difficulty in reconciling the details of Koolooa's find with Rae's accounts:

The origin of the cairn and encampment at Parry Bay does not appear to have been clearly established. It seems almost certain that Rae did not build the cairn. If his track-chart is compared with Hall's sketch-map, it becomes manifest that Rae reached a point about two miles to the southward of the cairn, saw the river on the south side of the plateau on which the cairn stood, but did not actually reach the plateau. Moreover, Rae did not state either in his original narrative or in his letter to the *New York Herald* that he had built a cairn at Parry Bay. Had he built one there he could not have failed to say so in the letter, especially if he had omitted to mention the fact in his original narrative – unless, as is not impossible, he had built one but had forgotten his having done so ... That Corrigal, unknown to

Typical Inuit summer tents with a circular floorplan
(Parry, *Journal of a Second Voyage*)

Rae, may have built the cairn is … unlikely, for Rae's narrative makes no mention of his having parted company with Corrigal during the short time that they spent at Parry Bay.[153]

It seems suspicious that it was only in his second letter on the subject that the sixty-seven-year-old Rae – thirty-three years after the event – remembered having built a cairn. Perhaps the old man, embittered by lack of appreciation and having developed an animus towards Hall, was determined to ensure that his achievements were noted, to the point of "appropriating" a cairn to which he had no claim.

Rae did not attempt to address the problem presented by the nearby "white man's" tent-site. That evidence was not only unsupported in his earlier writings but was specifically contraindicated. Having repeatedly noted that his party used snow igloos for shelter, Rae could hardly assert that he had erected a tent at Parry Bay. Yet Hall found very distinct traces of an oblong "white man's" tent, which measured 9 by 6 feet, the heavy corner stones weighing between 25 and 35 pounds. Hall repeatedly stated that "Koo-loo-a, Jo & Hannah are sure this tenting place was never made by Innuits. Jo & Hannah being well acquainted with White man's ways are so certain that White men had a Enct. here."

46

The Arctic literature is full of descriptions of circular Inuit tenting places.[154] The contrast with the oblong or rectangular floor plan of "kodluna" tents was as distinctive as the difference between Inuit soft-soled bootprints and the "long and narrow" footprints of the white men. Faced with the undisputed fact that Rae had had no tent at Parry Bay, Cyriax lamely concluded that "the evidence that the cairn and one of the tenting places were the work of white men is not fully conclusive. On these matters Hall accepted the opinions of Joe and Hannah, who would not have purposely deceived Hall. But they might have been mistaken."[155]

When in 1847 Rae and Corrigal left Cape Miles, they intended to return directly the same night and thus took "little or nothing to carry." But whoever built the tent was apparently burdened with quite a bit of gear, for near the tent was an oval of small stones, "where a pile of things that could not be gotten into the small tent was probably left – the stones to keep a skin cover over the pile."[156]

Rae was also unable to explain the mysterious buried "cache," and he therefore tried to cast doubt on its existence by referring to stories he had been told by the Repulse Bay natives about a depot left behind by the Ross expedition of 1830–34. He noted that "the description of the 'cache,' or depot," at the winter quarters of Ross's ship *Victory* "very closely agrees with Hall's mysterious depot ... being moved only across Boothia Gulf."[157]

Like all rationalizations of difficult Inuit testimony in preference to the accredited versions of white men, Rae's idea makes use of some unlikely premises. It presumes that Koolooa's cache, which had appeared to him "fresh" in 1854, had been built by Ross in 1833. Furthermore, Rae supposes that Koolooa was very confused about the location of this cache. Rae's suggestion that it was actually the Ross cache at Victory Harbour – on the other side of Prince Regent Inlet and sixty miles from Parry Bay – ignores the fact that Koolooa led Hall directly to the spot and that he knew it well enough to point out the cairn when it was still many miles distant and only observable to Hall through a telescope. Koolooa, as he said, was operating from personal observation when he pointed out the position of the deposit under the snow. Furthermore, his geographical knowledge was at least as good as Rae's, – he had correctly pointed out to Hall the discrepancies in Parry's chart of the northwest corner of Melville Peninsula. Again, Cyriax saw that this explanation of the cache did not work in Rae's favour, for it "thus shows that the cache at Parry Bay, if it existed at all, was not of [Rae's] construction."[158]

The details of Kia's story and the evidence of Koolooa's monument both convinced Hall that he was not hearing remembrances of Rae. He noted that all the natives who provided evidence were entirely familiar with Rae's two visits to their country and that they continually attempted to date the strange occurrences by referring to these visits. Nevertheless, it has been generally concluded that they had repeatedly mistaken Rae for an Indian or an unknown white man. Hall's alternative, that the man seen by Kia was a survivor of Franklin's ill-fated crew and that the monument at Parry Bay had been built to mark the passage of these men, was too far-fetched to warrant serious attention. It was far simpler to conclude that Rae, who was almost in the right place at almost the right time, had been the source.

But there were other "Etkerlin" seen on the Melville Peninsula and other relics recovered, and these cannot by any stretch of imagination be attributed to Rae.

~2~

The Etkerlin

MORE ETKERLIN

Kia's tale of his encounter with "Etkerlin" on the west coast was not the only one about strangers visiting the Melville Peninsula. In February 1868, Quasha and Kawonga told Hall that they had recently seen two white men near Igloolik. On further investigation, Hall came to believe their story because of its consistency. Quasha and his wife stated that they had seen these two white men at a place called Nelikiokbig, which they vaguely described as being "west of Ig-loo-lik." Luckily, on 17 April 1868, while travelling up Hooper Inlet, Hall described his route: "We begin to see the line of mountains – the particular high land we 1st see is *Nel-lo-ki-ok-big* where Quasher & wife saw the two White men."[1] Quasha and his wife had had further strange experiences:

Qua-shu & wife went over to Mel-o-kee-ta [Lyon Inlet] to see other Innuits on their return same fall when 1/2 way between Melokeeta & Tu-mee the dogs smelt something & tried to follow the scent. The day one of storm wind blowing & snow flying. On examination it was found that many fresh tracks of men were what the dogs were following – the foot marks of men with long and narrow feet – two men had on very long something on their feet wh. were sharp at both ends – wherever the snow was soft & deep these big tracks kept up the snow while those who had not these things all sank deep – tracks going toward the N.E. – very many had just been made for some plain not much snow in them.[2]

This undated event, with its graphic description of snow-shoe (ski?) marks, is puzzling. Parry's men explored the shores of Melokeeta/Lyon Inlet in September 1821 but did not proceed inland. On that occasion they met a small Inuit group, headed by the hunter Arnalooa,[3] and this encounter was well known to Hall's informants; more than forty years after the event, Hall interviewed a woman who had been a young girl in Arnalooa's party. Rae never approached the area.

After hearing about the two strangers seen by Quasha and his wife, Hall sent Tookoolitoo to a nearby village to interview Quasha's wife, Karwonga, about the strangers. Tookoolitoo returned with a full report, though this time the tale was not set at Nelikiokbig or Melokeeta:

In the fall … a party of Innuits went deer hunting at See-jok-big. Qua-shu [Quasha] wife & family Too-koo-lat [Too-goo-lat] & family & a good many more. All the rest of the Innuits but Qua-shu & wife Too-koo-lat & one old man a relation of Too-koo-lat stopped at Koong-wa (upper end of N. Pole Lake). There these the hunters killed a good many took-too. By & by Qua-shu & Too-koo-lat leave the old man & their families at Koong-wa & go on towards See-jok-big killing deer on the way. The old man & families move along slow following after then old man & women stop 1/2 way to See-jok-big from Koong-wa they left some skins & meat then next day Qua-shu's wife & Too-goo-lat's wife returned for meat & skins. Night before this return it snowed for the 1st time & some remained the next day. Got pretty near the skins & meat when Too-goo-lat's wife saw across the lake on E. side Etkerlin. The women were on one side & saw the Etkerlin on the opposite. Then by & by after seeing the 2 Etkerlin they went down the hill to get the skins & meat – there saw the tracks in fresh snow – the tracks very long & narrow Etkerlin tracks – then go home – going home hear a noise shouting very loud & they were most [of the way] home & they thought Etkerlin were killing the old man.

Then Too-koo-lat's wife asked the old man what he had been crying about for they found him all right – he said he no make any noise since they left him. Then the old man no sleep & women no sleep all that night after seeing & hearing what they did.

That night the old man shouting & crying all night to the Etkerlin praying them not be hard on them. The old man crying thus all night – "Anny-nurk-a-tu-nen-lu-e-wish-ee" – "We are cousins."[4]

Here we have a very definite geographical location. Seejokbig is well attested as being near the northern end of Miles Lake,[5] and Ooshoot described Koongwa as "the strait that unites N. Pole Lake and Christie Lake." The fear engendered by the Etkerlin was real, for the hostility between Inuit and their southern Indian neighbours is well documented. The anthropologist Kaj Birket-Smith noted, "It is characteristic of the relations between the Eskimos and the Indians that the former are always the superiors, particularly by virtue of their prosperity ... Not a few Chipewyan speak broken Eskimo, but no Eskimo lowers himself to speak Chipewyan. They converse with each other politely and use the term [Arnaqatiga] 'my cousin'; but no affection is observable."[6] The enmity was also noted by the Danish explorer and ethnologist Knud Rasmussen. He collected Inuit stories concerning Indian incursions into their land, and all the stories featured hostility and murder.[7]

In April, Hall met Ooshoot, the wife of Toogoolat, whom he estimated to be about twenty-five years old. Her father, Takeelikeeta, had been one of Parry's favourites.[8] Hall told Tookoolitoo to ask Ooshoot about having seen Etkerlin at Koongwa, and he waited anxiously while the two women conversed for many minutes. Eventually, Tookoolitoo "with joyous face" turned to Hall and said, "All right – she tells the same story as Kar-wong-un."[9] Like Karwonga, Ooshoot had vivid memories of her experiences at Koongwa. She remembered going with Karwonga to fetch "some meat & things they could not carry the 1st time & then after getting what they wanted they started back. By & by wanting to rest they sat down on a stone & soon Oo-shoo saw what she thought to be two Innuits & thought nothing particular of that till on resuming their walking they soon came to the tracks of 2 men which from their strange shape greatly frightened the women – the tracks of 2 men – of one large – tracks of the 2 narrow in the middle – & long." Ooshoot remembered the strange noise and the crying old man, and the fear she had felt that night as "they all slept in one tent then the wind blew a little in the night & shook the other tent a good deal & their dogs set up a terrible barking – the tent the woman & old man were in did not shake while the other made an awful shak-

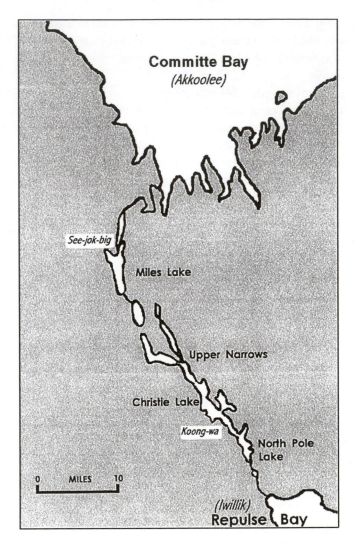

The Rae Isthmus, showing Koongwa and Seejokbig

ing noise. The old man went to crying out loud & kept it up all night saying to the supposed Indians that he was cousin to them."[10]

There was no doubt in the minds of any of the Inuit that the two women had seen the tracks of white men. Ooshoot noted that "when she came to Repulse Bay last year & 1st saw Kob-lu-na tracks she at once began to think about the tracks she & Kar-wong-un saw near Koong-wa for the tracks appeared the same kind – long & narrow in the middle – & the toe such square across."[11] The "shouting noise" is also significant; to the Inuit, the white men's speech was loud and discordant, and was often described as similar to the barking of dogs.

This was not the only strange encounter Karwonga and Ooshoot had with strangers in this area:

By & by three women go pick fire wood Molasses' wife [i.e., Quasha's wife, Karwonga] Took-goo-lat's wife [Ooshoot] & one other woman – by & by they pick fire wood & start to go home then Qua-shu's wife stopped to fix her bundle of fire wood for a string had broken. The other 2 women kept on walking on by & by the woman behind could see them for they had gone down a hill.

Qua-shu's wife the woman behind walked on & soon a little one side of her over ahead she saw a head pop up & down from behind a big rock. She came along & now & then a head would pop up & withdraw. She thought it to be one of the women who had gone ahead & when she near she cried up "I can see you." She had got back a few steps when she saw the two women her companions treading on abreast & then she became frightened for she knew she had been greatly mistaken in thinking that one behind the rock to be one of the women – on telling Hannah this she said "if you don't believe it ask Too-goo-lat's wife."

Qua-shu's wife was awfully frightened & threw off her pack right away & ran as hard as she could after the other women who were not far from the tent.[12]

Although one cannot be sure, the two incidents mentioned above seem to have occurred within a short period. The Inuit were so disturbed by them that they decided to move towards Lyon Inlet to continue hunting. Later in the season, while returning to the south, they again saw the Etkerlin:

Good while after all [the above] the men were out side of the tent (the ponds & lakes partially frozen up & Took-too hunt closed) to get meat & Tood-noo; by & by while eating one of the party saw two Etkerlin on the other side of the lake by wh. they were – they (the E.) were seen to pass along southerly & after a while coming to an arm of the lake where they could not safely pass they turned back & after a while did not see them move again. They were watched till dark.[13]

While passing through the area in March 1869, Hall noted that "right close by on the bank w. side of the Narrows [which connect

North Pole and Christie lakes] Jack's wife points out the exact place where she & husband & Qua-sher & wife were enct. for a while when soon after they removed up the lake ... She says the men In-nuits on their return to this place saw the strangers going up she points in a south direction from where the Enct. of the Innuits of her party had been here."[14]

A later story tells of an even more frightening interaction be-tween the native hunters and some strangers. In 1893 Captain George Comer, a veteran whaling captain, heard the following from a native called Sick Sick (probably Shiksik – "squirrel"):[15]

Old Sick Sick told me that when he was a boy he went Deer hunting with his Father they shot a Deer and before they started to skin it two very large men came to them and one of them put the Deer on his back and then both went away. Sick Sick said they did not talk but were unusual large men. With a pencil he drew a rough drawing of the scene and then told me that his legs shook till the two men were gone his Father offered no resistance. I wondered at the time if these two men might not have been survivors of the Franklin Expedition as Sick Sick would have been a boy at that time.[16]

There is corroboration that strangers had passed through the area without concern for the property of the Inuit. Quasha's wife Kar-wonga informed Hall of a theft of some material from native cairns:

By & by all the Innuits (some Neitchille men – there among them E-nook-poo-she-jook [Innookpoozhejook] of the number) moved along this way toward I-wil-lik (southerly) travelling as Innuits do men ahead women & children following. The men going ahead tho[ugh] good way off from Koong-wa they saw a great smoke rising from there. As the party got a lit-tle further on toward Koong-wa they saw 7 men walking [illegible] now & then hid behind hills among wh. the 7 men were travelling. When they got to Koong-wa the Innuits found all the meat & all the fire wood that be-longed to Qua-shu & Too-goo-lat gone – they found a fire place close by where the 2 piles of meat had been. The fire-place was inside of a Took-too Look-out such as made for Innuits to stand or sit in as may be to watch deer wh. way they are coming from & going to. This wall high. The fire place inside this & made by 2 stones for kettle to sit on – using the wall for back of it. Here where the meat had been cooked – the kettle must have been moved for so all the Innuits thought on account of the appearance of the marks of smoke on the stones. The 7 men Etkerlin as seen by the party of Innuits were dressed in clothing looking black as [illegible]. There was good deal of meat in the 2 piles. Qua-shu's pile had 2 saddles & good many carcasses of deer & Too-goo-lats had a lot of meat & there was a big pile of fire wood (Andromeda) close by.[17]

Again, Ooshoot partially confirmed Karwonga's tale, remarking that although she personally knew "nothing about the loss of the deer meat & fire wood," she had "heard that winter that they were gone by the hands of some strangers."[18] Ooshoot noted that "a great deal of Et-ker-lin seen & talked about all that summer & fall when she & party were at Koong-wa & See-jok-big"; and Karwonga noted that after these frightening encounters with strangers, there was "trouble all the time about the Et-ker-lin losing something & things changed – no one going out alone – Women pick fire wood somebody go with her – no man go hunting alone."[19]

Astonishingly, when Hall interviewed Toogoolat, the hunter said he did not remember having been robbed or having seen seven white men – but he then said that his wife might remember! Toogoolat did, however, agree that about that time there was "much talk about Indians being about & seen & that 2 women saw what they thought were Indians."[20] This was probably a case of the often-noticed reticence of the male hunters, who were reluctant to talk of their experiences and thus "foolishly waste" hunting or resting time. Hall repeatedly remarked that the women were much more communicative.

On first glance, it seems probable that all these white men seen on the Rae Isthmus near Repulse Bay must have been members of one or other of Rae's expeditions. However, a closer look at Rae's journals is required. Although Ooshoot would have been very young in 1846 when Rae first came to Repulse Bay, Rae and his men repeatedly passed Christie Lake on their exploratory journeys. On 29 July 1846, after shooting a buck, Rae and one man went to a nearby ridge to spy out the terrain. Returning at 8 P.M., Rae sent out two further parties, of two men each, to explore the nearby territory. On 1 August he saw nearby the "recent tracks of two Esquimaux on the sand." Rae's *Narrative* clearly indicates that he knew and was known by the Inuit encamped at Christie Lake at that time, though it was evident, as he noted, that "we had not yet wholly gained their confidence."[21]

On 2 August 1846, Rae found a native encampment with one tent, where he met an old man, Iliak, and his wife, Reiluak. They told Rae that the remainder of the party were out hunting musk-ox and that this hunting party consisted of "two sons and their wives."[22] The sons were named Nokshuk and Ivitchuk. The latter was well known to Rae, since he later served as his hunter and guide.[23] Clearly, this was not the same encampment and hunting party that Hall heard about from Karwonga and Ooshoot, for the details do not match. In their case, the hunt was for caribou, not musk-ox, and those remaining in camp were the two young women and Toogoolat's aged stepfather – not an elderly couple.

After leaving the old couple, Rae dispatched three men back to Repulse Bay. He and his remaining three men then spent from 5 to 13 August 1846 near Christie and North Pole lakes, looking for fishing places and buying dogs from the Inuit. He came upon the native encampment on the tenth, on "a small point about eight miles up Christie Lake" from the narrows, and found that "our friends were delighted to see us."[24] He bought four of their best dogs. The next spring, Rae and his party again travelled over the narrow isthmus. They stopped at Christie Lake on 5 April, and the following day they found two acquaintances, Shimakuk and Kei-ik-too-oo, camped nearby with their families.[25]

It seems reasonable that the tracks of any of these small groups of men could have been seen by Ooshoot in 1846–47. Yet Rae's account makes it abundantly clear that he was well known to the natives whom he encountered there, most of whom had seen him at Repulse Bay. In addition, he was always accompanied by a native interpreter – at first Ouligbuck (Mar-ko) and later the aforementioned Ivitchuk. Ivitchuk remained in the North with his people, and he would easily have been able to identify the source of any of Rae's footprints to those Inuit who did not see the men themselves.

If Hall's estimate of Ooshoot's age was correct, Rae's second expedition of 1854 would be a more likely source of the sightings of the strange white men. Rae and his six men arrived at Repulse Bay in August 1853 but found no Inuit there. After an uneventful winter, Rae planned on "buying dogs from the natives for sledge work, but no Esquimaux were to be found, although Ouligbuck and two of my half-breeds were sent to places forty or fifty miles distant to search for them."[26] Leaving half of his men at Repulse Bay, Rae took the others with him during his spring explorations, and he first encountered Inuit when he was westward bound in Pelly Bay. He again met these natives, along with others, on his return to Repulse Bay at the end of May. Hall learned that the Inuit were quite familiar with Rae and his activities:

Mam-mark has been telling us this evening something about Dr Rae. She says, in answer to my enquiry, how many men made up his party when here the last time, "Three men were left here, while Dr Rae took with him to Pelly Bay & beyond four including *Mar-ko*, the interpreter (whom Dr Rae miscalled 'Oo-lig-buck')." This exactly agrees with Dr R's account.[27]

In their travels to and from Castor and Pollux River during the spring of 1854, Rae and his men passed Koongwa but apparently did not encounter Inuit. As with his journeys of 1846–47, the same considerations apply when trying to identify Rae and his party as the protagonists of the Inuit stories of Etkerlin. Rae and his men were well known and liked by the natives of the area; Rae remarked that while at Repulse Bay in 1846–47, he and his men were "surrounded by native families" and that in 1854, while on his journeys, he was "in constant communication" with the natives.[28] It is thus most unlikely that he and his men would have been mistaken for strangers.

In view of what we know of Rae's expeditions, the most incongruous incidents to be explained would be those in which the Etkerlin stole meat from the Inuit and their caches. In 1846–47 Rae and his men were so successful at their hunting that although originally provisioned for only four months, after fifteen months in the field they brought back one-quarter of their original supplies. "By our own exertions," wrote Rae, "we procured food for twelve months."[29] He also stated: "We succeeded in procuring sufficient supplies for all our wants without aid from the natives, from whom we did buy some food in the spring, but only to give it back gratuitously to them afterward, with additions, when they visited us."[30] Rae's group did even better in 1853–54:

I found the three men who had been left in charge of our property quite well, living in abundance, and on the most friendly terms with a number of Esquimaux families, who had pitched their tents near them. The natives had behaved in the most exemplary manner; and many of them who were short of food, in compliance with my orders to that effect, had been supplied with venison from our stores … In the early part of July, the salmon came from the sea to the mouths of the rivers and brooks which were at that date open; and we caught numbers of them. So that occasionally we could afford to supply our native friends with fifty or one hundred in a night … We had still on hand half of our three month's stock of pemican [*sic*], and a sufficiency of ammunition to provide for the wants of another winter."[31]

This description of Rae's circumstances makes it inconceivable that he or his men would have been forced to pilfer a deer from a frightened hunter or to despoil Quasha's and Toogoolat's caches. Rae did admit to having opened, out of curiousity, a native cache of stored clothing, but he added, "Of course we repacked the bale."[32]

Another point is that Rae's route on his various travels was well known to the natives. When Hall passed over the same ground in 1869, his companion Eek-choo-ar-choo ("Jerry") pointed out where Rae had camped & fished near Committee Bay.[33] On 31 March of that year, when Hall crossed a river called Kee-goo-wi-ark, south of Cape Weynton, the Inuit told him that "here Dr Rae had an enct. & made a deposit of provisions when on his 1st journey in 1847 & had an enct. here again in 1854."[34] It is impossible to read Rae's accounts of his travels and imagine him wandering back and forth looking for a way to cross a lake, playing hide-and-seek with Inuit women, or stealing meat from two native caches.

Ooshoot noted that "she was young at the time & does not well remember about what was seen & what took place when at Koongwa," but she confirmed that Karwonga was "a very truthful woman & can tell about the matter."[35] The consistency and detail of their stories point to the fact that the women were telling of real encounters. So if these tales do not seem consistent with Rae and his men, we again must wonder who these strangers could have been.

Predisposed as he was to hear about Franklin survivors, Hall became very excited when told of a "great deal of Etkerlin." He believed that the seven men seen near Koongwa must have been of the same group that was later seen farther north on the Melville Peninsula. What he most wanted was some direct evidence linking these strangers with the white men who had abandoned their vessels near King William Island.

From all of this apparently consistent testimony Hall could draw only one conclusion: "I am almost certain he [Kia's stranger] was a white man – even more, that he was one of a party of white men that had found their way in a boat from the low land (Simpson Peninsula) near Pelly Bay, across Committee Bay to Fury & Hecla Strait."[36] Hall had learned of the strange encounters at Koongwa before he set off for the Melville Peninsula. On his return later in the year, he was even more convinced that these strangers were the necessary link between King William Island and the Etkerlin seen at Nelikiokbig and Parry Bay. When telling the natives at Iwillik of his Melville Peninsula discoveries, he was to learn of further connecting clues.

Apart from his two close friends Tookoolitoo and Ebierbing, none of the Inuit had as much contact with Hall as Ouela did. Almost from the moment he was landed ashore by the whalers until the time he left Repulse Bay to return to the United States five years later, Hall, who had nonchalantly been "adopted" into this hunter's family, relied on Ouela's advice and support. At times Hall praised Ouela, describing him as "a man that would command respect, honor & admiration in civilized lands for his truly eminent, genuine & inherent virtues."[37] But he could also remark, "What a double souled Innuit is Ou-e-la! In him is apparently, at times, a good heart – but in the interval, there looms up in him the very *devil* himself!"[38] In late 1868 Hall was casually talking to Ouela when the stories concerning strange white men were mentioned. These stories had an interesting effect on the old man:

All at once *Ou-e-la* said he now recollected something he had not thought of for several years ... He said that a long time ago when ... sledging along on the ice of Repulse Bay ... they came to fresh foot prints in the snow of 2 men & a dog. The tracks of the men showed long feet & that they toed out like those of the white men they had seen when Dr Rae & party were at their encampment near Beacon Hill when here with two Boats [1846 and 1847]. The tracks of both men were long – longer than any Innuits but the tracks of one man much longer than the tracks of the other man. The shape of the feet-prints were same as those of white men of Dr Rae's people but there were no deep heel prints – that is no heels on the boots. All the Innuits were certain these tracks were not of any Innuits. They were greatly surprised at seeing any such tracks & thought it must be they would find white men somewhere about the Bay & therefore kept up a sharp look out for them after that but did not see any more tracks like them nor did they find any white men though the Innuits were sure they must be about not far off.[39]

Hall felt that "Ou-e-la's testimony of to day in fact goes largely to confirm some of the incidents related by Ka-woon-ga"[40] concerning the encounters near Koongwa/Christie Lake. Ouela returned to this subject in a further interview two days later, adding certain details and making minor corrections:

The tracks were not fresh, but had been made some time – perhaps in the middle of the winter as he says, but they were completely defined so that the Innuit party followed them for a distance equal to the distance from our present Ig-loos to the sea shore which is about 1/2 a mile. The foot prints appeared to have been made when the snow was soft that is after it had freshly fallen & the subsequent gales had swept the unimpacted snow about the foot prints away leaving them raised & very distinct … [The tracks] of the larger man were extremely long which showed to all the Innuits who saw them that the man who made such long [illegible] in his steps could not be otherwise than in good condition – that is could not be poor & starved … The tracks showed that the men had come from the land to the northward & westward & had passed onto the ice of the small Bay there. Some of the Innuits of the party thought that they would find the white men who they were sure had made these tracks as well as perhaps many others (whites) at Mel-loo-kee-ta (Lyon's Inlet) … but were greatly disappointed on getting to Mel-loo-kee-ta finding no Kob-lu-nas (Whites) there.[41]

Hall was amazed that Ouela, who had been his host for almost four years, had never mentioned this encounter before. Although it is impossible to fix the location of this incident exactly, the similarity between the descriptions given and the modern Inuit names near Cleveland Harbour and Southeast Cape indicate that this is the general area being spoken of.[42] Ouela had corroboration for his story, for the same tale was told by an old lady named Eveeshuk.[43]

The association of white men's tracks with those of a dog is suggestive when we recall that Kia and Koolooa also had seen dog tracks beside those of the white men. According to Ouela, these tracks "were same as those of white men of Dr Rae's people but there were no deep heel prints," which implies that Rae's men wore heeled boots, although Rae himself was known to prefer soft soles. The fact that the tracks were without heel prints, like those seen by Arkootoo on the west coast and unlike those seen by Kia and Koolooa, is therefore inconclusive.

In late May 1869, Hall heard another tale of strange footprints:

Kob-big now tells a story about the tracks of 2 sledges & a good many men
as having been seen on the land main land bottom of s. termination of Pelly
Bay ... these *tracks were seen* – seen by an Innuit by the name of Mong-er ...
The tracks seen to lead from the big island in Pelly Bay & afterwards seen
on Shartoo (Simpson's Peninsula). The Innuits all have thought & now
think that these tracks were made by white men for it was determined that
no Innuits, neither of Pelly Bay, Neitchille nor of Oot-ke-ish-e-lik had made
them. Two Igloos were seen that this stranger party had made & occupied
no platform for bed made in these igloos – only the floor – the snow blocks
showed how they had been cut out with different kind of knives from what
Innuits in this part of the country use – apparently cut with same kind of
knife I have given to Kob-big (Hudson Bay dagger).[44]

Even after his years among the natives, Hall could not understand
how his friends, all of whom knew very well that he sought information about white men, could have been so unnaturally reticent
about these sightings. He admitted that "it seems strange to me
(but not so much so as it would once, before I had learned how singular a people Innuits are) that Koong-ou-er-lik never told us a
word about this before when we saw him for months in 1866."[45]

Rae, again, is the only non-Franklin candidate for this tale,
though the description of the site is not specific enough to be ad-
vantageously compared with Rae's track of his journeys in Pelly
Bay. Rae and his men made extensive use of sledges and igloos,
though the fact that the latter were built without a sleeping platform is curious, for Rae was well acquainted with this architectural
feature and its utility.[46]

ARTUNGUN

In addition to his interviews with Koolooa and Kudloon about Kia's
encounter on the northwest coast, Hall was told very consistent stories about strange white men who had travelled in the eastern and
interior regions of the Melville Peninsula. An old man named Artungun, his wife Arnalooa, and their son Koopa (whom Hall had
previously interviewed at Repulse Bay) provided most of the testimony. This was amply supported by the other natives present.

Traditionally it has been believed that these recollections relate to activities of the crews of HMS *Fury* and *Hecla*, which visited the area under the command of Captains Parry and Lyon. After wintering their ships at Winter Island in 1821–22, Parry and Lyon sailed up the eastern coast of the Melville Peninsula to the vicinity of Fury and Hecla Strait. They spent the next winter among the Inuit at Igloolik. Throughout their stay in the Arctic, the men of the *Fury* and *Hecla* had extensive contact with the Inuit and were well remembered as cheerful and generous friends. Many of the stories told to Hall related to the activities of Parry's crew, and they attest to the accuracy of the Inuit memories. Yet the Inuit made it plain that their memories of other "Etkerlin" were unrelated to Parry and his men.

Hall's older informants remembered Parry and Lyon well. Toolooarchu recalled that the white men had wanted to take him back to their own country, a fact confirmed in Parry's *Journal*.[47] Hall's primary informant, Artungun, who had been a child at the time, told of his visit to the white men's ships.

Ar-tung-un … remembered Parry and Lyon, both of whom he said were very fond of little children. Lyon, he recollected, had danced [with] the little ones, and sung nursery rhymes to them. Ar-tung-un himself could sing several songs learned from the sailors, and could count in English. He said that he was once dead on board Parry's ship, and was brought to life by Parry's an-ge-ko [shaman, i.e., the ship's doctor] bleeding him, and he showed Hall the scar on his arm made by the lancet.[48]

Many sick Inuit were treated by Parry's doctors, so many in fact that, at Igloolik, Parry had a small hospital built on the ice to prevent overcrowding of his ship's sick bay. Artungun's recollection of being treated on board is therefore important, for a few days before construction of the hospital Parry mentioned that a "fine little boy" named "Attangut" was brought aboard for treatment "apparently in a dying state."[49] There can be little doubt that Attangut/Artungun were the same person. Artungun's wife Arnalooa also remembered the visit of the *Fury* and *Hecla*. Since Hall described her as "of Parry fame," it is probable that she was the same individual described by Parry as "a pretty young woman of nineteen or twenty."[50]

When Hall arrived in the Arctic forty years after Parry's departure, Artungun was an elder of his band, respected by his peers and wise in the ways of the world. He and Hall exchanged names in the Inuit manner, and Hall was quite proud to be known as

"Artungun," while Artungun revelled in his new name, "Mitter Hall." Throughout his notes, Hall's respect and affection for Artungun are manifest, and he had no doubt that his friend was telling him the simple and unvarnished truth.

Ar-tung-un says many years ago ... many natives were then stopping at a place called Ing-near-ing up a large Bay to the N.E. of Ig-loo-lik where one night in the fall of the year just before the time for snow the dogs commenced barking furiously when many Innuits sprang out of their beds & went out of their tents to see what was the cause. Some four or five Et-ker-lin (Indians) were seen passing along each conveying in his hand something like a stick. It was not so dark but that their figures were distinctly seen cutting sharply the back ground which was the sky. Ar-tung-un was not one of the natives that saw these Indians for he was too late getting out of bed but not thinking it possible that there could be any Kob-lu-nas about he thought the strangers must be Indians. The Innuits were all so frightened that the next day they removed from Ing-near-ing to an island Ki-ki-tuk-che-uk ... The distance to Ing-near-ing 2 *sleeps or 3 days* from this Island, N. oo-glit.[51]

The exact location of Ingnearing is in doubt, since Artungun's description (or Hall's understanding) was not very clear. There was a place of similar name (today's Ingnerit) on the shore of Baffin Island that was truly "to the N.E. of Igloolik" in the vicinity of Steensby Inlet.[52] The walrusing place at the north end of this bay was described to Hall (by Armou) as "Ing-nier-ring," the name being derived from the stone found there, which was used by the Inuit "in striking fire."[53] No known exploring party of whites approached this part of Baffin Island during the appropriate period. Another similarly named place is Ingnertoq, which is on the eastern Melville Peninsula near Amitoke and South Ooglit Island. This identification would require that Hall had mixed up his directions, for Ingnertoq is southwest of Igloolik (that is, Hall may have been told that Igloolik was northeast of Ingnearing). Nevertheless, this deserves consideration because of Ingnertoq's proximity to the location of other sightings near Amitoke.[54]

Although exact identification of Ingnearing is impossible, as is the identification of Nelikiokbig (where Quasha and Karwonga saw two white men), it is evident that these encounters with "Etkerlin" took place in areas never visited by Rae and that these tales must therefore refer to some other party of white men. And these were only two of many connected incidents:

The next spring following the great fright by the Indians [at Ingnearing] Ar-tung-un & many Innuits went deer hunting on the main land (near Og-big-seer-ping above South Oo-glit Isle). The two men or natives Ar-tung-un & an Innuit now dead Al-er-gaite were walking along when all at once they heard the *bang* of a gun as Ar-tung-un thought for he had heard guns fired many times when Parry & Lyons' ships were at Ig-loo-lik – then looked around to see what made the noise & by & by heard another gun report when they saw the smoke as of a fired gun not far off arise from behind some land & immediately 2 took-too (deer) came running swiftly from that same place from whence they heard the gun & saw the smoke. Then Ar-tung-un & his companion were terribly frightened & ran to their tents & at once removed their families from the main land to south oo-glit by the means of their ki-as … Never saw anything more of those Et-ker-lin.[55]

Artungun and Alergaite were not the only Inuit to conclude that some strangers had been hunting on the mainland to the west of the South Ooglit Islands. Armouyer also had some interesting per-sonal recollections from a hunting trip to the interior:

Ar-mou-yer & an Innuit by the name of *Ak-ke-che-uk* … were off on the High Land westward of Am-i-toke on a deer hunt in the fall of the year. They were up on very high land when there was still much snow – hard snow (ou-ye-too) really glacier ice as Joe says & they were walking along side of it when they saw something on the ou-ye-too. Ak-ke-che-uk was walking ahead & Ar-mou-yer directly behind following after. It looked like took-too *ar-nuk* (deer droppings) when they went close to it. Ak-ke-che-uk 1st got close to it when he called to Ar-mou-yer to come to him & look at it.

They saw at once that it was human dung & had been dropped there but a little while. The color of it was very light not of the dark appearance usual for Innuits. The 2 Innuits talked the matter over & could think of no Innuits that could have been about there but Innuits living by the salt wa-ter side among whom was Ook-pik … Ook-pik & the other Innuits were there tented down near the salt water & they [Armouyer and Akkecheuk] thought it possible that they might be up on the High Land deer hunting but still the very light color of the *ar-nuk* (human dung) made them think it could not be from an Innuit. They examined this *ar-nuk* very closely for there was something about it that looked singular to them. They never had seen any Innuit *ar-nuk* like that before.

After that they went about their business of deer hunting & that day saw a great many deer tracks but couldn't see any deer. The tracks all fresh but no deer. These tracks of took-too (deer) they saw were on the ou-ye-too (fresh water ice) covered with hard snow, but they didn't see any human tracks. The sharp toes or hoofs of the deer would make & leave marks in the hard snow while any men walking on the same would not leave any tracks at all. Seeing so many deer tracks (or sharp hoof marks) in the hard snow places (a great many of which is there among the high land about there) & not seeing any deer made them Ar-mou-yer & Ak-ke-che-uk think there must be some body about there hunting deer & frightened them away.

After a few days hunting succeeding the day they saw the singular looking *ar-nuk*, in which hunt they were successful in killing quite a number of deer, they returned to the salt water side & there saw Ook-pik & his family & the other Innuits. They found to their surprise that none of the other Innuits had been off deer hunting anywhere about or in the locality where they had been. The subject of the *ar-nuk* Ar-mou-yer & Ak-ke-che-uk had seen on the *ou-ye-too*, the strange look it had – the many deer tracks they had seen that day without seeing any deer was there talked over by all the Innuits there tented by the salt water side westward of Arn-i-toke & they all knew then that there must be strangers hunting in the High Lands.[56]

The strange looking *arnuk* remained a mystery for many years. Then, during the winter of 1866–67, Armouyer met his first white men "when he arrived at the Ships Harbor Island at the time 4 American Whalers were wintering there" and instantly recalled that the strange droppings "at the ships had the same appearance."[57]

The evidence for the presence of white men in both Artungun's and Armouyer's stories was circumstantial. In yet another story the strangers were actually seen, as Hall relates:

One time (not a great while after the above [that is, not long after Artungun and his companions heard the gun and saw the two fleeing caribou]) Ar-tung-un & Al-er-gaite went deer hunting at the same place where they went deer hunting before together when they heard the gun reports & saw the smoke at the last report. The particular place Ar-tung-un now marks out on Parry's Chart & he shows the place to be by one of the two or 3 small lakes that extend to the westward of the very large lake I discovered & passed over last year on my return to Repulse Bay from Ig-loo-lik [Tes-su-e-ark, now Hall Lake]. The place is near the lines of mountains Parry has upon his Chart & on a parrallel [*sic*] with Og-big-seer-ping or as Parry calls it – *Agwiperwik* [Parry's chart actually shows it as Agwisseowik]. They killed 2 deer & made a cache of them & returned to their tents when they sent 3 boys after them.

The boys were Koo-pa, In-nu & Ki-a (the latter (Ki-a) Innuman's brother) A correction; *Al-er-gaite* was the one who returned to the tent 1st that is he got back before Ar-tung-un for the latter remained out over night – to watch a deer that he had shot with an arrow which remained sticking in the deer's side. Al-er-gaite was the one that sent the 3 boys after the 2 deer. When Ar-tung-un got back the boys had returned – they the boys had returned without the deer meat – had left the meat dogs & all for they had seen 4 Et-ker-lin near where the 2 deer had been deposited. After the deer had been put apart upon the backs of the dogs & a part prepared & put upon their the boys own shoulders they saw upon a hill not far off 4 Et-ker-lin each with something like a stick in his hand & heard a noise like foxes then great laughter. The fox-noise & great laughter the boys did not hear until they had thrown away everything & were running away. Before the boys ran they saw the largest or tallest one of the Et-ker-lin who was very tall make motions with his right hand which was raised high over his head. The motions were swinging motions from the North toward the South. Soon as the frightened boys got back & reported what they had seen the Innuits were all alarmed & the lifting stone was resorted to which said the 4 strange beings were not Et-ker-lin.[58]

The white men's strange laughter and harsh "fox noise" (remembered as "shouting" by Karwonga and Ooshoot at Koongwa) had clearly frightened the young boys. As always, Hall attempted to verify this story by cross-examining other witnesses. He had previously interviewed Koopa, and he now met Innu, who with typical native reticence had said nothing of the incident when listening in Artungun's igloo. When Innu again arrived in camp he was closely questioned by Hall:

Knowing him to be an Innuit who was of the party of the three boys who saw the reported four Et-ker-lin many years ago I raised my head from my couch & asked him if he had ever seen any *Et-ker-lin*. He answered quickly *"Na-o"* (No). Following this he hesitated a moment & then corrected himself & said many years ago He & Ki-a & Koo-pa together when after some deer meat where some deer had been killed saw *three Et-ker-lin*. He then most earnestly & most eloquently described the incident which description was precisely the same (save a few minor points) as Koo-pa had told me at Repulse Bay short time before starting on this journey.[59]

In a later interview, Innu added more detail:

One time long ago In-nu – Ki-a & Koo-pa went after some deer meat. When they got there they saw three (3) men on the top of a hill close by – they had such clothes on that they shook very much in the wind – they all were sure they were not Innuits but thought them to be Et-ker-lin. In-nu so frightened he cannot remember what these men had in their hands. Cannot tell whether the clothes were light or dark. The place near the high land West of Arm-i-toke. Between the large lake (Tes-su-e-ark) & the high land w. of it ... Soon as he (In-nu) & the other boys saw these Indians they threw away their deer meat leaving the dogs with meat on their backs & then ran with all their might for home.[60]

The evidence seems clear. Artungun had heard shots and seen frightened caribou; Armouyer and Akkeecheuk had seen *arnuk* and the evidence of someone hunting in the highlands; Innu and his two companions had actually seen (and been seen by) the frightening creatures. Even so, there is no direct linkage between these three or four men and the seven seen near Koongwa by Toogoolat's party when returning to Iwillik (Repulse Bay).

All of the events described by Artungun occurred to the west of Amitoke, in an area consistently and clearly described as between the big lake and the mountains, far from the areas explored by Rae. There are two more stories, again from Artungun, to investigate. Throughout his tales – at Ingnearing where he was late getting out of bed, with Alergaite when he only heard shots, and again when he tracked a caribou and missed the three boys' encounter – Artungun never met the strangers who were hunting in his land. These tales are therefore (well-informed) hearsay. But the old man did have personal encounters as well.

THE DOG

The various tales of Etkerlin are geographically separated, yet the descriptions relating to Koongwa, Iwillik, Amitoke, and Parry Bay nevertheless have certain common features. Perhaps the most curious and perplexing is that of the white men's dog. Ouela and Evee-shuk saw the tracks of three men and a dog in Repulse Bay, and Kia and Koolooa saw the same tracks near Cape Englefield. Near Ami-toke, Koopa and his friends saw the three or four men. Only Artun-gun actually saw the dog:

Ar-tung-un says that a few years ago he was out hunting at Kee-gee-wee a place little back of the line of mountains that run north or westward of Am-itoke – on a parrellel [*sic*] of am-i-toke when two frightened deer ran swift-ly by him. Soon a large grey dog came swiftly on their track which the dog followed by scent. When the dog saw him (Ar-tung-un) it stopped. As Ar-tung-un was about to fire an arrow at the beast (the dog) he saw that a short string was about its neck when he carefully unbent his bow & tried to coax the dog to him Kob-lu-na way. The dog appeared playful but was too shy to allow Ar-tung-un to catch hold of the string. The dog was following the deer *from the North* & when Ar-tung-un had tried to catch the dog it ran away to the N.W. as A[r-tung-un] shows on Parry's chart. The dog had short hair & it did shine very much something like the one of the dogs Parry & Lyon had though larger. It had short ears. String short only touched the ground. His curiosity so excited about the strangeness of the dog he did not notice *what kind* of string it was about the dog's neck … The dog a very small body long thin legs & poor the tail long & curving up-wards just like the one Parry had only much larger. That is the dog was the same build or structure or form, but while Parry's was black the dog he saw with string about its neck was grey – like in color one of mine which old See-gar let me have, grey. "Jo" says it surely was a Grey hound from Ar-tung-un's description … Ar-tung-un says they had three dogs on board Parry & Lyon's ships. Ar-tung-un having said this I turn to pages 297 & 299 of Lyon's Private Journal & see that there was a large Newfoundland dog – a greyhound belonging to Parry & a terrier "Spark" belonging to Reid on board of the Fury & Hecla.[61]

Since the dog was on a leash, it was obviously a white man's animal. The description, as Ebierbing (Jo) noted, does seem to fit a greyhound, and it has led most historians to conclude that it was in fact Parry's dog (anachronistically called a "greyhound" by most writers, though it was described by Parry as "of the breed called by game-keepers buck-dogs").[62] Yet Artungun's testimony shows that he knew Parry's dogs very well, as Hall recorded:

Parry's dogs on the ice (Parry, *Journal of a Second Voyage*)

For the purpose of testing the memory & accuracy of old Ar-tung-un I asked him to tell me about the little dog which was on board of Parry & Lyon's ship. He said the little dog was a great favorite with everybody & was a spotted one. One time a wolf came about the ships & this little dog with Parry's dog which was a black one ran after the wolf when several white men hastened after the dogs to bring them back. After awhile the men returned bringing Parry's dog but they could find nothing of the little pet dog so all concluded that the little dog must have been killed & eaten up by the wolf. Next day (continued Ar-tung-un) some of the white men went out to see if they could find out what really had become of the little dog. When they returned they brought the head it being all that they could find of the little dog. He could not remember the name of this dog but on my telling him it was "Spark" he then smiled & said it sounded just like it. The old man has not only told the facts about this little dog – a terrier – as related by Lyon whose work I have with me but has told this much more that the dog was spotted & that its head was found.[63]

Artungun's comment that the dog he saw was "just *like* the one Parry had" implies that he was sure that it was not Parry's dog itself. Artungun's friend Armouyer also knew of the encounter with the dog. He remembered that "Ar-tung-un didn't think at first, that this was a dog & was about to shoot it with an arrow when he saw a string on its neck & then he thought it a dog of the same kind he had seen on board of Parry's Ship when at Ig-loo-lik which had long legs & a very small body with short hair."[64]

To clarify the situation, Hall specifically reminded Ar-tung-un that Parry had owned a greyhound, and Artungun confirmed that he remembered this as being true. Confusingly, though, Artungun remembered that "while Parry's was black, the dog he saw ... was grey." This is corroboration that at least in his own mind Artungun was sure that two separate dogs were being spoken of. It should also be noted that the colours mentioned are not conclusive, for "greyhounds" come in various shades. Artungun described the dog he saw as having "a very small body, long thin legs and poor, the tail long and curving upward," which does seem to be a tolerable description of a greyhound. When combined with the statement that it was "of the same build or form" as one of Parry's dogs, this seems conclusive. Artungun noted that the dog "looked very much like the animal in shape which the dog is chasing in the illustration in Parry's work ... only the dog had a long tail."[65] In Parry's illustration, all three of the dogs from the ships are shown frolicking on the ice, and the one being chased is undoubtedly Parry's greyhound, well drawn and with a noticeably short tail.[66]

Parry's greyhound never strayed far from the ships and could not have been seen to the west of Amitoke. But in 1823 a small party was led by Captain Lyon on an exploratory mission to the area. This mission will shortly be investigated in detail, but here it is sufficient to note that Lyon used "ten excellent dogs, which he had taken great pains to procure and train."[67] This is clear evidence that they were Inuit dogs, well suited to the rigours of overland hauling. There is no evidence that any of the three pet dogs carried on the *Fury* and *Hecla* were ever in this area. Thus, the "white man's" dog seen by Artungun, like the "white man's" tenting place seen in

Parry Bay, remains an inconveniently specific detail that cannot be related to Parry or Rae.

THE CAMP

Old Artungun not only saw the dog on the leash and heard white men shooting near Igloolik, but he found some relics of white men. Like Koolooa, he concluded that they were "fresh" when he found them. These relics, since they could not possibly be attributed to Rae, were assumed to be even older:

The old woman Ar-na-loo-a of Parry fame ... says that she was with her husband many years ago when he was hunting deer not a great ways from the mountains west of Arm-i-toke. He was on one side of a pond & she walking on the opposite side. Her husband found a tenting place at the foot of a mountain close by the pond. He found there a large oot-koo-seek painted red & a tin canister of same color & he saw half of another plate down in the water of the pond. There were strong indications that salmon had been cooked in the large tin can for there were salmon bones about the can. Everything looked fresh as if done not long before for there was no moss or rust about the tin cans. Yet she & husband thought no one could have left these things there but Parry or some of his men ... There was a fire place of stone by the tent place. She saw these things soon after Ar-tung-un found them. *Arnalooa* saw the tenting place near the foot of the mountain by the lake of the party that must have left the cans and made the fire place. This mountain is some distance to the – of the wall of mountains that extends far to the Northw– back or west of Arm-i-toke.[68]

Hall had already heard of this campsite from Artungun's son Koopa, and he was pleased that Artungun's wife confirmed the story. The next day Hall interviewed Artungun himself about this campsite.

Ar-tung-un was hunting took-too one summer a long time ago, one day's travel from the line of mountains estward [*sic*] (nearly on a parrallel [*sic*] with the point where Lyon turned back when seeking to find a Pass through the mountains to the western sea in 1823) when he came to where there had been a tenting place – the shape of the tent as shown by the stones that had been used to fasten it down square or oblong, long & narrow. It was not such a tent as the Innuits use. The particular spot near base of a mountain & along side of a small lake.

Along side of the lake he found an oot-koo-seek about 1 foot by 15 inchs [*sic*] & 18 inchs deep as shown by Ar-tung-un's measuring with his hand on Parry's Chart. It was tin & painted red – completely enclosed except a hole in the top of about 3 inchs diameter. Inside were some pieces of salmon bones. Besides this oot-koo-seek he found a round can about the size of a tin kettle hanging by our fire lamp & this was painted red too. No top to this but there was some very white tallow in it. Never saw any cans painted like this on Capt Parry's or on Lyon's ships. This can was painted all over on the outside while those on Capt Parry's & on Lyon's ships were painted only on the tops. Never saw any of the large cans like the square one described above on board Parry's or Lyon's ships painted red all over on the outside. All painted only on the tops with letters on the tops.

On the other side of the fresh water pond found an earthen stone jug that is as "Jo" say a jug like one Ar-men gave me some seal oil in a little while before we left Repulse Bay which was an earthen stone jug of light color. This jug that Ar-tung-un found had its top broken off. These cans that Ar-tung-un found were not rusty nor was there any moss about them – was very much surprised at the freshness of every thing about them for he certainly thought that nobody but Parry or some of his ships companions could have tented there & left those things. Along side of the tenting spot was a fire place of 2 stones & which were blacked with smoke. The fire that had been used was the *Est-shu-tin* [Andromeda tetragona] for a little of it was there in a little pile by the fire place. Everything looked as though it had been done only a little while before. The smoke on the stones would not have been there on simply burning Est-shu-tin more than 2 or 3 years & the wood would have been white & looked very different from what it did in less time says Ar-tung-un.[69]

Once again, this tale is seemingly consistent. The description of the tent site as "shown by the stones that had been used to fasten it down square or oblong, long and narrow" is reminiscent of that found by Ebierbing and Tookoolitoo in Parry Bay. It was undoubtedly a site used by white men. Hall continued:

Ar-tung-un does not now think it possible that these things could have been left as he found them by Parry or his men for the salmon meat that he found in the large red can would have been gone & everything else would have looked altogether much older than they did. Koo-per [Koopa] the other 2 natives with him saw the four Et-ker-lin before Ar-tung-un found these things. The place where the Et-ker-lin were seen was not far from where Ar-tung-un found the tenting place & the things now described. Thus much has Ar-tung-un told me as a man speaking without any thought of deception. I can read the man like a book. He means to tell the truth & only the truth.[70]

Artungun had observed that the relics were fresh: the firewood unweathered, the salmon remains undecomposed, and the smoke marks from the fire looking as if they were not "more than two or three years" old. Although not particularly clear about when these things had been found, Artungun continually referred to the event, not in terms of Parry and Lyon in the 1820s, but with reference to the visits of Rae twenty to thirty years later. But Rae never penetrated the Melville Peninsula – he confined his explorations to the western shore – and he never mentioned fishing while on the march. Since Rae had not approached the area (as Artungun well knew), modern historians were forced to conclude that these relics were left by Parry's men in the 1820s.

There was another white man's campsite found at a place called Kingmetokebig. Hall reached this spot on 6 April 1868, noting that it was "close in to land N. of a point called Kong-mung." This was undoubtedly near present-day Kingmitokvik Point, four miles north of the modern village of Hall Beach.[71] According to Papa, there was a tradition that Parry's men had camped there and killed ducks, but Hall noted that "the story of Innuits that Parry had tent at King-me-toke-big not confirmed by old Ar-tung-un who saw Parry & Lyon."[72] Hall specifically "asked Ar-tung-un if Parry or any of his (Parry's) people ever had a tent or a party at King-me-toke-big for the purpose of killing ducks in the summer or for any other purpose. He said 'No.' The reason some Innuits think so is because some beads [crossed out in original and replaced by means of a caret with "beans"] & what was conjectured to be a Kob-lu-na tenting place were found there. Ar-tung-un said Parry & Lyon used to have hunting parties stationed at Ar-lang-nuk but not farther south."[73]

Again, it is impossible to account for a white man's campsite on the coast in the vicinity of the Ooglit Islands from the records of any known explorer. Parry and Lyon twice passed the point in their ships – when sailing northbound en route to Igloolik on 16 July 1822 and when sailing southbound on 14 August 1823 – but on neither occasion did they land any personnel.[74] As was the case with

Koolooa's monument and Artungun's strange dog, the internal details of Artungun's campsite have been ignored by the historians.
By his own admission, Artungun did "not think it possible that
these things could be left as he found them by Parry or his men."
Even so, the standard opinion has been that this early expedition
was the only source of these things, for no other white men were
known to have approached the area before Hall.

Arnalooa and Artungun were maddeningly vague about where
the ootkooseek had been found, mentioning only that it was inland
from Amitoke. Amitoke is easily identified, for it is a prominent
and well-known landmark on the eastern shore of the Melville
Peninsula. A projecting headland that is sometimes spoken of as an
island because of its singular appearance in relation to the low land
around it, the Amitioke Peninsula lies roughly halfway between
Repulse Bay and Igloolik. Of course, reference to this large peninsula does not adequately define the geographical area of Artungun's find, but other clues in the Inuit testimony allow us to locate
the white men's camp with some exactitude.

As Artungun told Hall, "the place where the Et-ker-lin were
seen [by the three boys] was not far from where Ar-tung-un found
the tenting place"; Innu described this place as "near the high land
West of Arm-i-toke. Between the large lake (Tes-su-e-ark) & the
high land w. of it." As Hall recorded, Artungun gave even more
details when describing the nearby spot where he and Alergaite
had gone hunting the year before: "The particular place Ar-tung-
un now marks out on Parry's Chart & he shows the place to be by
one of the two or 3 small lakes that extend to the westward of the
very large lake I discovered & passed over last year on my return
to Repulse Bay from Ig-loo-lik. The place is near the lines of mountains Parry has upon his Chart & on a parrallel [sic] with Og-big-
seer-ping or as Parry calls it – Agwiperwik." With such precise geographical clues that are related to Parry's own chart, we should be
able to determine whether any of Parry's crew did in fact reach the
highlands where the mysterious Etkerlin were seen.

Only one detachment of Parry's men need be considered. In 1823
Captain Lyon of the Hecla, having heard from the Inuit of a route
leading to the west coast of the Melville Peninsula, took a small
party in search of it. Leaving the ships at Igloolik on 7 June, Lyon
and two companions, Alexander Gordon (Greenland mate) and
George Dunn, set off with a sled that weighed 191 pounds and was

loaded with 1,200 pounds of supplies. The three men first proceeded along Quilliam Creek, then turned south along the eastern side of the mountainous spine of Melville Peninsula. They were looking for the opening which the Inuit had assured them would lead to the west coast. Lyon's description of his trek is frustratingly laconic. He wrote that "nothing can be more uninteresting to readers of Journals than a long detail of courses and distances,"[75] which admittedly is true in most cases, though one might wish in this particular case that he had been less considerate of his public.

The weather was atrocious throughout the journey. Gales and deep snow confined the men to their tent for whole days, and when they emerged to struggle on, they found that the plain on which they walked was "as completely and as deeply covered as in mid winter," forcing them to "absolutely wade" through the drifts, where "the dogs sunk to their bellies at every step." Lyon wrote: "I have seldom passed a more dreary time than this; for the sun being at this season always above the horizon at midnight, and yet not being seen on account of the snow, caused a continual and most fatiguing glare, extremely painful to the eyes: our view was limited to about 100 yards; and this, with the discontented whining of our dogs, was altogether tormenting beyond expression."[76]

Lyon soon realized that he had somehow missed the pass through the mountains which the Inuit had told him about, but with characteristic determination he continued to the south in the hope of finding another. His track, as laid down on the chart accompanying Parry's *Journal*, shows that the three men reached a point about thirty miles to the north of Amitoke on 19 June and then began to retrace their steps northward. If Lyon and his men were the inspiration for the Etkerlin seen by the Inuit, they must have been seen during the period 15–24 June 1823. To assess whether this was the case, we must turn to Lyon's account of his travels for that time.[77]

There are definite points of similarity between the Inuit recollections of the Etkerlin and the inland excursion of Lyon, Gordon, and Dunn. The three men saw many caribou and, although not involved in a hunt, they killed at least three of them. Lyon remarked that the "constant whining and fighting of our dogs ... invariably drove every thing from us," which calls to mind Armouyer and Akkecheuk's observation, while hunting in the highlands, that "there must be some body about there hunting deer & frightened them away." Lyon and his two companions often travelled at night, and this could tie in with the encounter at Ingnearing, where the Inuit "sprang out of their beds" to see "four or five Et-ker-lin" silhouetted against a darkening sky. Their shots could have been heard at any time, and their *arnuk* found.

Unfortunately, comparison of Lyon's journey with the geographical clues embedded in the Inuit testimony of the campsite's location is inconclusive. As indicated by the route marked on Parry's chart and reconstructed from the physical clues on a modern topographical map, Lyon's campsite of 19 June, about which he laconically stated only that they "moved over the plain to the foot of the mountains, and there tented," may have been the one found by Artungun. It is certainly within ten miles of it.

Also of interest is the fact that Lyon spoke of an incident with a dog. On 21 June he remarked that his party was detained "in consequence of one of the dogs slipping his harness and giving chase to a couple of deer, which he pursued into the mountains with great spirit, and was soon out of sight, regardless of all our cries to stop him." This dog was given up for lost, but a few hours later was found "tracking our footsteps, and coming back much fatigued." At first glance, this incident seems convincing and conclusive. It occurred in the correct general area, and the remainder of the dog's harness could have been the "string" which Artungun noted around the strange dog's neck. However, as previously noted, Lyon's delinquent sled dog was not Parry's greyhound but was one of those procured from the Inuit, and it is hard to believe that Artungun would not recognize the animal as an Inuit dog.

Were it not for the "freshness" of the finds, it could be easy to assume that the campsite discovered by Artungun had been made by Lyon and his companions. But even then, there would be other discrepancies between Lyon's account and Artungun's recollections. To conclude that Artungun confused the campsite with one of those made by Lyon during his travels ignores the fact that Artungun knew Lyon's route very well and would presumably have been unsurprised to find relics along it. Artungun specifically told Hall that he found the white men's tenting place "nearly on a parallel *with the point where Lyon turned back when seeking to find a pass through the mountains,*" thus showing a complete familiarity with Lyon's movements.

Even more to the point, Lyon's recalcitrant dog pursued his solitary adventure on 21 June 1823, whereas Artungun insisted that he saw his "white man's" dog thirty years later. If Artungun was the "fine little boy" named "Attangut" who was treated at Igloolik on 3 February 1823, he could hardly have become a mature hunter and seen Lyon's dog five months later.[78] Moreover, when Artungun found the white men's encampment, he was accompanied by his wife Arnalooa. But according to Parry's *Journal*, when Lyon's dog slipped his harness Artungun's future wife, the "pretty little" Arnalooa, was married to "a very little man named Koo-il-li-ti-uk, nick-named by the sailors 'John Bull.'"[79]

There is also a discrepancy regarding the seasons. Rae journeyed up the west coast of the Melville Peninsula in May 1847, Lyon down the interior in June 1823, and both men experienced heavy snow and gales, which made their travels difficult. By contrast, Kia and Koolooa's recollections were of a time when the snow was off the ground. Similarly, the Etkerlin at Ingnearing were seen, according to Artungun, "in the fall of the year just before the time for snow." He heard the shots of the caribou hunters "the next spring" and saw his dog during the "same summer" that Kia saw his stranger. Similarly, Armouyer and Akkecheuk conducted their caribou hunt in the Amitoke Highlands "in the fall" and specifically stated that there was "still much snow – hard snow (ou-ye-too) really glacier ice" on the ground. Lyon did not find snow that was hard; the snow was so soft that he had to "wade" through it. It should also be noted that the *arnuk* which the two hunters found on this hard ice had been dropped only "a little while" (a frustratingly inexact phrase), and Armouyer was certain that it had been found one year after Artungun saw his strange dog.

Although it is not prudent to base firm conclusions on the inexact terms that white men use for the seasons in the Arctic, great reliance can be placed on Inuit descriptions of snow conditions. All the incidents involving active interaction – seeing the Etkerlin pass by, finding the dog, meeting some waving and laughing strangers – were described as occurring during the "summer" or "fall"; that is, "before the time for snow." None of the Inuit witnesses mentioned gales or inclement weather, features that loomed large in both Rae's and Lyon's accounts.

One final point concerns the tin canister of fish remains that Artungun found. By the time Lyon and his two companions returned to their ships on 26 June, there had been many occasions on which they could have deposited a converted can at a lakeside encampment. But, as a careful reading of Lyon's account shows, the weather was so uniformly bad that he and his men would have been most unlikely to have eaten any freshly caught fish – unless they had braved the fierce snowstorms and hacked their way through the thickly frozen lakes, activities that are not mentioned in his journal. Significantly, Lyon does not even mention seeing any Inuit during this trip, and he certainly does not mention laughing and waving at three frightened boys!

Despite these difficulties, Cyriax voices the modern opinion that "Artungun's account of the place where he had found tins and other relics suggests that these had been left by Captain Lyon."[80] As was the case with Rae on the west coast, Lyon can be seen to have approached the appropriate area and to have engaged in appropriate conduct so that he could have been the source of the Inuit stories. But, again in parallel with Rae, Lyon did so during the wrong time of year and during the wrong year. With Rae, the discrepancy in time was seven or eight years, significant enough but not beyond the realm of possibility when Inuit dating techniques are taken into account. With Lyon, this difference was more than three decades, and the stories were told by a man who had personally met Lyon when he was a little boy. In regard to both cycles of Etkerlin stories, the Inuit were remarkably consistent, dating each encounter as having occurred during the decade 1847–57. So the next question to be explored is, Could the Inuit appreciation of time really be a generation out?

RED CANS AND BLACK BEADS

Artungun gave another clue about the campsite's builders by describing the paint scheme of the cans. He was very specific, stating that the ootkooseek was "painted red ... Besides this oot-koo-seek he found a round tin ... and this was painted red too ... Never saw any cans painted like this on Captain Parry's or Captain Lyon's ships. This can was painted all over on the outside, while those on Captains Parry and Lyon's ships were only painted on the tops, with letters on the tops."[81]

At first glance, this detail seems significant. If Artungun's assertion is correct, perhaps we have the clue we are seeking in trying to identify the depositor of the relics near the lake. Especially intriguing is the fact that the Franklin expedition's cans, which were sup-

plied by Samuel Goldner, were invariably painted red![82] But
unfortunately the matter is far from straightforward. An innovation
of the Napoleonic Wars, tinned food was apparently taken to the
Arctic for the first time on Parry's first expedition in 1819. The supplier for that voyage was the firm of Donkin and Gamble, which
was also contracted to provide the same product for his second expedition in 1821. Parry never mentions the paint scheme employed
by Gamble, and it may have varied between different canned products. Some of Parry's tins have survived to the present day, including some previously unopened ones, which were found to contain
perfectly preserved beef. One tin, supplied by Donkin and Gamble
and originally containing "carrots and gravy," was found to have
been "painted, probably by the packer, with a light yellow paint."[83]

By the time of Parry's third expedition (in 1824), other firms were
competing for the tinned food contracts. The firm of Morrison prepared 510 pounds of "portable soup," and James Cooper of
Clerkenwell petitioned to be allowed to supply part of the preserved fresh provisions.[84] Apparently, Parry felt that each firm –
Donkin and Gamble; Morrison; and Cooper – should provide one-
third of the total he required. However, there is no confirmation
that this policy was approved or carried out. Nor do we know
whether Morrison or Cooper had supplied part of the tinned food
of Parry's earlier expeditions. But it is unlikely that they did. In his
Journal, Parry specifically mentioned only Gamble.[85] It is interesting
that two of these three firms later supplied canned products to other Arctic expeditions and that surviving tins from that time indicate
that Cooper's (then Cooper and Aves) cans were painted white
while those supplied by Gamble were blue.[86]

Thus, the evidence of the "red cans" is at best inconclusive,
though it is encouraging that the Franklin tins supplied by Goldner
were the only ones known to have been painted red. Artungun was
not the only Inuit hunter to find them:

Net-tar says that many years ago she her husband & several other Innuits
were tented at a place called See-er-wa-ark-chu which as pointed out to me
by both Net-tar & Pe-oong-ee-too on Parry's excellent chart of his discoveries is about 2 miles west of the entrance to the Narrows leading into Murray Maxwell Inlet. Her oldest son Ar-che-ar-chu was out one day near their
tenting place when he saw a mouse running about & finally it darted under a large flat stone. He lifted this stone to find the mouse that he might

kill it. He didn't find the mouse but to his great surprise he found a tin canister which was a little over 6 inches in diameter & 8 or 10 inches in length as shown by pantomime by the old lady's hands.

There were 2 cans as the old lady now says & were painted red both of the same size … Now she tells me by the aid of Hannah the contents of the tin red canister which her son found when hunting for the mouse (ou-er-nuk). One spoon, 1 fork with 2 prongs & the handle of this fork was something like oo-ming-muk (musk ox) horn – 2 small tin cans some 4 inches high & 3 inches or a little more in diameter as shown by her hands & these painted red on the outside like like [sic] the large canister in which the things were … Also was in the large can a piece of saw plate about 2 1/2 inches wide & 6 inches long – no teeth on this saw plate & also, a thin piece of iron which Hannah says must have been a piece of hoop-iron.

There were besides the above a *great many black beads* all without being strung, were loose in the bottom of the canister. Bottom of the canister not only covered with them but there was considerable depth of beads. There were 2 long red beads among the black ones & these 2 red ones the only other kind of beads, in the canister. The string of black beads having the 2 long red ones she (Net-tar) gave me just as she left off talking with me (on the 23rd) are all what came from that canister. There were no other red beads but the 2 she gave me. Lying outside of the big canister was a long flat file & the stone which had covered the canister had covered the file. She saw everything just as found at once on her son finding them, for the spot was along side of the tenting place – & other Innuits of the party saw them too. They all looked around hoping to find more things of same kind but failed in finding any more.[87]

Again, a quick check of Parry's chart reveals that this coastline to the west of Murray Maxwell Inlet (modern Murray Maxwell Bay) was visited by his men. But this is not conclusive, because it is unlikely that white men would cache a used can, some loose beads, and some cutlery. It is more probable that Archearchu found a deposit of white men's "gifts" that had been left for safekeeping by some other Inuit. Being only a few miles from another campsite at Gifford Fiord, made by Lieutenant Hoppner in 1823, it seems reasonable that these relics originated on Parry's ships. Hall seems to have confirmed this when he continued his interview with the old woman: "Had you Net-tar ever seen black beads among the Ig-loo-lik Innuits before your son found the black beads he did as described to me? Answer, that *she had*. Were the beads of exactly the same kind as your son found? Answer that *they were*. Where did those black beads you 1st saw – that is the beads you saw before your son found those he did. – come from? Answer. *From Parry as the Innuits told her* (Net-tar)."[88]

It would be easy to conclude that this correlation between black beads and red cans shows that both came from Parry's ships. But, again, things are not quite that simple. Hall remarked that the "Innuits know the distinct history of even minute things they possess."[89] We know that Parry, like most explorers, was quite generous with beads, which he found to be highly prized by the Inuit women. He noted that Arnaleeia's wife had "the front of her jacket adorned with numberless strings of beads that we had given her,"[90] and he remembered giving a woman named Ablik a "very large present of beads."[91] The Inuit later gave Hall a string of seventy-three beads, half blue and half white, and they told him that all but two of these had come from Dr Rae, who had given them to the natives of Repulse Bay. The other two were Franklin relics. They also were white but were somewhat larger than the Rae beads and had parallel sides.[92] Another single white bead that Hall was shown had been presented to the Inuit by Ross at Victory Harbour in 1832. It is perhaps significant that none of the beads from these other expeditions were black.

Hall found that Parry's beads were remembered. Hall recorded: "Kou-lou [Kia's sister] here gives me a little string of beads, ½ of them red & the rest white & says that they were from Parry when he was at Ig-loo-lik longtime ago. One little blue bead of this lot of beads was not from Parry but is one of some beads that I gave to a woman at Ig-loo-lik when there the 1st time I visited there winter before the one just passed."[93] Kou-lou's beads show that Parry, like other explorers, distributed beads of different colours. (It should be noted that Net-tar did not actually remember having seen black beads on Parry's ships but that "the Innuits told her" they came from there.)

If the bead colours are inconclusive, what of the red cans? Parry left the Inuit a large quantity of empty tin canisters at Winter Island, and he often gave these valuable articles as presents.[94] However, he fails to mention the colour (or colours) of the cans. There remains the possibility that some Inuit combined treasures from different sources, putting Parry's beads in canisters obtained elsewhere. Again, we cannot confirm the Inuit testimony by reference to the physical evidence. Although Parry may have had red cans, Artungun never saw them on Parry's ships. The only surviving example was painted yellow, and within a few years Parry's supplier was providing blue cans. Similarly, although Parry probably gave out black beads, the only evidence we have from a recipient indicates that he distributed red and white ones.

It should also be noted that Murray Maxwell Bay is about half-way between, and almost in a direct line with, Nelikiokbig and In-gnearing (if located in northern Steensby Inlet). As always, Hall hoped that chronology would help: "How long ago since these things were found? Found a long time after Dr Rae was at I-wil-lik the 1st time. Her son Oong-er-luk at the time the things were found was of the age as the girl standing before us. (This little girl, Hannah thinks, may be about 9 or 10 years & Oong-er-luk as I & Hannah both think may be 25. This if true in the estimate, would make the time of finding the things about 15 years ago)."[95] This estimate of the date of discovery (1853) is similarly inconclusive. A depot of Parry memorabilia could have been made by an Inuit at any time after 1823, and it is not impossible that a well-hidden cache of valuables could have lain undiscovered for thirty years. The fact that the discovery was dated in relation to Rae's first visit is nevertheless interesting, and the date 1853 will emerge again.

We cannot prove that Parry's tins were red or that his beads were black, though the evidence suggests that either or both could be true. If so, it is likely that the relics at Artungun's camp were left by Lyon and his men on 19 June 1823, as has generally been concluded, regardless of how unspoilt the salmon appeared to be or the freshness of the smoke-stained rocks and nearby wood. But while it seems possible that the physical evidence might fit, the testimony and chronology cannot. A sick little boy does not grow to manhood in a few months. He cannot, in the same space of time, raise his own son to boyhood and send him off to fetch the carcass of a slain deer. He may find an old campsite and be fooled into thinking it is recent, but he cannot miraculously metamorphosize into a mature married hunter and challenge a strange dog while hunting deer. These changes all point to a period fifteen to twenty years after Parry and Lyon left Igloolik.

TIMING

Rae remarked that "the great difficulty with the Esquimaux is to obtain correct dates and numbers."[96] Despite this problem, Hall spent much effort in trying to determine both the absolute and relative chronology of the events the Inuit described. He found this to be a frustrating endeavour with a people to whom exact dating was completely alien. Not that they didn't try. When Hall asked Koolooa to date the discovery of his cairn, he took fifteen minutes to arrive at an answer. Armouyer and his friends laboured for thirty-five minutes on a similar task. But we must not lose sight of the fact that these Inuit were being asked, from memory alone, to date events that had occurred at least fifteen to twenty years earlier. Many of them were children at the time of the encounters. Under such conditions, it is perhaps unrealistic to demand unvarying consistency.

Much precision is not really required, however. The traditional view allows only four alternatives for the various Etkerlin stories: that they were about Indians, not white men; that they were total fabrications; that they were recollections of the visits of Rae (1846–54); or of Parry (1821–23). The internal details of the stories seem to rule out encounters with Indians, and it is extremely unlikely that total fabrications would have had such details as the sound of white men's voices, the shapes of their bootprints (both with and without heels), and the colour of their vegetable-diet *arnuk*. The most likely non-Franklin alternatives, and those that are almost universally endorsed, are that the Inuit tales are garbled memories of the Parry and Rae expeditions. Consideration of these visits does not require that the natives remember events to the exact year; more important is that they apply to the correct generation.

The most unlikely date for the various Etkerlin experiences emerged from Quasha's story of seeing two white men at Nelikiokbig. Hall originally thought that this encounter had taken place in 1860.[97] Quasha and his wife Karwonga were also involved with the Etkerlin at Koongwa. Karwonga remembered that these incidents occurred "six years after Dr Rae went away when here the 2nd time."[98] This again gives a date of 1860, and the clear implication is that Karwonga believed the two events to have occurred in the same year.

In an effort to corroborate Quasha's dating, Hall asked Armouyer whether he had ever heard of Quasha and his wife meeting with two white men at Nelikiokbig. Armouyer could not give an exact date, admitting that he had only heard of Quasha's encounter recently, but he did give the useful information that Quasha had gone deer hunting at Nelikiokbig "that same fall that Ki-a saw the strange man."[99] He further elaborated by noting that "there was a great deal of trouble among the Innuits at Ig-loo-lik that winter following the fall when Qua-sher went deer hunting at Nel-li-ki-ok-big & that a man of Qua-sher's relation got killed during that trouble."[100]

Hall, persistent as ever, next interviewed Kia's friend Kudloon, who concluded that Quasha and his wife had gone hunting "nine summers the coming summer."[101] Hall felt that Kudloon's date (1859) was close enough to Quasha's to be taken as corroboration. The "great trouble" that descended on Igloolik the year after the strange encounters of Kia and Quasha is a common theme of many of these stories. In-nu's wife Six-e-en told Hall in 1868 that it had been "9 winters including this" since "there was trouble at Igloolik." Hall concluded, "This agrees within 1 year of the time when Qua-sher & his wife saw the 2 white men."[102]

With all of this apparently consistent testimony, Hall might have felt justified in accepting the date of the encounters as sufficiently demonstrated. Yet in subsequent interviews he tried to refine the date of Quasha's experience. Quasha made use of the familiar method of counting out years by significant events. He noted, for example, that he "had seen Dr Rae at Pelly Bay seven years after his first visit to their country," which is exactly right and refers to Rae's visit of 1853–54. Quasha then said that he "had remained at Iwillik seven winters and a half," which Hall added to 1854 to get 1862. Quasha's last statement was that "Rae went home from his second visit; after which they went to Ig-loo-lik, and two years later, saw the kob-lu-nas." Hall therefore calculated thus:

Quasha sees Rae 1854
Quasha remains at Iwillik 7½ years 1854–1862
Two years later see Etkerlin 1864

Quasha's ambiguous statements are illustrative of the problems encountered in trying to pin down Inuit chronology. Are we to add the "two years later" to the year that Rae went home (giving 1856) or to the time when Quasha and his wife went to Igloolik (in 1862)? Hall accepted the second reading, remarking that "it brought the story down as late as 1864."[103] This was in character for Hall, who had come to the Arctic in 1864 with the hope that some Franklin survivors would still be alive.

After meeting Koolooa and Kia's sisters, Hall realized that he had a problem. When Koolooa had found the cairn on the west coast of the Melville Peninsula, he had thought it was fresh. According to his estimate, this occurred in either 1854 or 1855, and it was determined that Kia had seen his stranger that same year (according to Koolooa) or the year before (according to Kudloon). Arkootoo claimed that her brother had seen his stranger "several" years after Rae's departure (Hall understood her to be referring to the second departure – 1854). But the preponderance of evidence was that Kia's encounter could not have been as late as 1864 or even as late as 1860.

Let us look again at Quasha's chronology. The problem seems to lie in Hall's addition of the seven-and-a-half year stay at Iwillik to the year of Rae's departure. Yet a simple change of Hall's punctuation would give a very different reading. By slightly changing the wording and punctuation (the original Inuit recitation, of course, had none) we get: "They had seen Dr Rae at Pelly Bay seven years after his first visit to their country. [They] had remained at Iwillik seven winters and a half. Rae went home from his second visit, after which they went to Ig-loo-lik and, two years later, saw the kob-lu-nas." In this reading the only sentence with chronological significance is the last, and it gives a date of 1856 for the encounter at Nelikiokbig. This is only one or two years later than Koolooa's date for Kia's sighting, with which it is linked in Armouyer's testimony.

It could justifiably be argued that this variant date seems to disregard Karwonga's apparently specific statement that the two Etkerlin were seen "six years after Dr Rae went away when here the 2nd time." It is perhaps significant to note that Parry indicated that "Esquimaux are no great proficients in the science of arithmetic, their numerals extending in general only to five, and then commencing again."[104] He notes that "Attow-seuk" can signify either "one" or "six." If we substitute "one" for "six" in Karwonga's statement, we get the more amenable date of 1855. It should perhaps be kept in mind that Hall's notes are themselves edited versions of Inuit testimony. Karwonga may have ended her statement at the word "away," and the "when here the 2nd time" could be Hall's gloss. If Karwonga was actually speaking of Rae's first visit (1847), then the resultant date for the encounters at Koongwa (1853) would be much more appropriate for Franklin expedition survivors.

We can reconcile the absolute chronology given by Quasha and his wife only by assuming that either they were mistaken in telling it or Hall was mistaken in transcribing it. Although we can see plausible sources of error and possible corrections, we can justify modification of their recorded testimony only on the basis of inherent improbability. No white explorers were active in the central Arctic between 1858 and 1864, and the whalers had not yet penetrated the relevant areas. Whether referring to Franklin survivors or to Rae, the dates require lowering by at least five years.

But Quasha and Karwonga were not the only witnesses. Artungun's experiences are also difficult to date precisely, though they confirm that the Etkerlin's visits had been closer to the time of Rae's visit than to Hall's. Artungun told Hall that he saw the strange dog "before Dr Rae came to I-wil-lik the last time,"[105] and he tied this event to Kia with the statement "that it was the *same summer* that Ki-a saw the strange man over near Adge-go (Fury & Hecla Strait).[106] Artungun continued to link together his experiences. He noted that it was "not a great while after" the incident at Ingnearing that his son Koopa and the other two boys saw the Etkerlin when recovering the dead caribou[107] and stated that "the time the 4 Et-er-lin seen by Koopa & the other 2 boys was after Dr Rae was here 1st time as Ar-tung-un thinks & remembers."[108] He further remarked that Koopa and the other boys were frightened by strangers "not long before" he found the white man's campsite by the lake.

Artungun's direct statement about when he found the camp is less straightforward: "The time when he found [the campsite] was before he heard of Dr Rae being at I-wil-lik the 1st time. He heard of Dr Rae being at I-wil-lik the next summer after Dr Rae left which was in 1847 … Koo-per [Koopa] & the other 2 natives with him saw the four Et-ker-lin before Ar-tung-un found these things."[109] Since Artungun could not refer to Rae's visits by calendar years, we must presume that Hall took the "first time" to refer to Rae's first visit and thus added "which was in 1847." Combining this with Artungun's statement that "he heard of Dr Rae being at Iwillik the next summer after Dr Rae left," Hall concluded that Artungun found his camp in 1848. This was too early for Hall's purposes: the *Erebus* and *Terror* were not abandoned until April of that year, and even Hall could not accept that survivors had come as far as the Melville Peninsula in only one season of travel. This anomalously early date also confounded the dates derived from other witnesses.

As with Quasha's testimony, the problems Hall had with Artungun's statement may have been largely self-inflicted. Even in English translation, Artungun's statement "before he heard of Dr Rae being at Iwillik the first time" is ambiguous and could just as easily be understood as "before he first heard of Dr Rae being at Iwillik." This allows a different result: Artungun could now be speaking of Rae's second departure, of which he heard the next year (1855). It would have been some time shortly before this that he found the campsite. This would accord with his other testimony.

Although this reconstruction brings Artungun's testimony more closely in line with that of the other Inuit, it still creates problems. If the relics were, as Artungun thought, two or three years old, and if they were seen after 1847 but before 1855, we would have a time of deposition of 1851–52. Artungun's statement that he saw the dog "before Dr Rae came to Iwillik the last time" (in 1854) is consistent with this, the implication again being that the hunters in the highlands were encountered between Rae's two visits to Repulse Bay.

Hall was apparently unconcerned that he seemed to have two separate and consistent chronologies. The Kia encounter, according to Kia's companions and relatives, occurred after Rae's second visit with the dates centring on 1855. Yet the encounters described by Artungun, which according to him were contemporary with Kia's stranger, were dated by him between the Rae expeditions of 1847 and 1854. The original Quasha chronology implied 1859–60; the "corrected" chronology of his wife Karwonga resulted in 1853. Who was right?

It is possible that a seven-year-old cairn could appear "fresh," but human dung is another matter. Armouyer noted that when he and Akkeecheuk found the strange *arnuk*, it "had been dropped there but a little while." When asked to date his hunting trip, Armouyer linked his experience to Artungun's and assured Hall that he saw the strange *arnuk* "one year, that is the next fall after Ar-tung-un saw the *strange dog* chasing 2 deer."[110] This relative chronology was encouraging, but Hall persevered in trying to get Armouyer to arrive at a specific year. Armouyer, Papa, Nukerzhoo, and Koopa spent thirty-five minutes recalling incidents and discussing chronology among themselves until they all agreed that Armouyer's hunting trip to the highlands had taken place "TWO WINTERS AFTER DR RAE WENT HOME WHEN HERE THE LAST TIME – the following summer they saw the strange looking *ar-nuk*."[111] Hall summarized the chronology as given by Koolooa, Artungun, and Armouyer:

Now ... by the testimony of the noble hearted, ever to be remembered Koo-loo-a, the time when Ki-a saw the strange man (one of Franklin's lost companions as I believe) was in 1854 ... Now it is well known in the civilized world that Dr Rae left Repulse Bay in *1854* – then it was in *1856* – in the summer or fall that the 2 deer hunters, Ar-mou-yer & Ak-ke-che-uk, saw the ar-nuk that they determined could not be of any of their people ... Ar-mou-yer's testimony is that this ar-nuk was seen the next year after Ar-tung-un saw the strange dog – the dog that was not of the Innuit breed – then it was in 1855 that the strange dog was seen by Ar-tung-un. Now by Ar-tung-un's last testimony he saw the dog the same year Dr Rae left Repulse Bay when here the last time which of course makes it in 1854. By this there is a difference & disagreement of one year between the testimony of Ar-tung-un & Ar-mou-yer.

Perhaps Ar-tung-un intended to be understood that the time when he saw the strange dog chasing two deer, was the same year that he heard at at [sic] Ig-loo-lik of Dr Rae's last departure from Repulse Bay which news he heard in the spring of 1855. If so then the two accounts agree. I must here record my great confidence in the testimony as to time in Ar-mou-yer's story told to night. He took much time & labored hard in determining his answer to my questions: & there cannot be a question raised as to his good memory & intended truthfulness by any one who knows the man.[112]

Hall was now convinced that he had the truth. He realized that his original estimates of the Etkerlin encounters had been in error by a few years, that the white men were seen the "same summer" as Kia's stranger, and that this was now firmly fixed as 1855. His certainty would not last, however.

The Inuit testimony of various encounters at Koongwa indicated that these were separated from each other by weeks or months rather than years, so the theft of Toogoolat and Quasha's meat was also linked to Kia. It is therefore interesting to note that "the time when the party was stopping at Koong-wa & lost their tuk-too & saw Etkerlin was before Dr Rae came to Repulse Bay the last time – it was a long time after he was there the 1st time." Further evidence that this occurred before 1854 was Ooshoot's statement that "same fall [of theft] Too-goo-lat & wife left I-wil-lik for Igloolik & did not see Dr Rae when at I-wil-lik last time."[113]

Other Inuit also remembered that their experiences were bracketed by Rae's two visits. Ouela said that he had seen the white men's tracks in the ice of Repulse Bay "in the spring of the year & two years before Dr Rae & party came here the last time. The last time he added, Dr Rae & his men came here with only one boat, which is a fact."[114] Ouela thus dated the incident to 1852, and he did it by referring, correctly, to Rae's visits. It cannot be ignored that Ouela was well acquainted with Rae, for by his own admission he had met Rae on both of his visits to Repulse Bay.[115] Ouela referred Hall to his stepmother Eveeshuk for corroboration of this date.

Eveeshuk was even more explicit in her chronology than Ouela had been. In either 1846 or 1847 "she had seen Dr Rae & his men when here" and this had been "a long time before she & the other Innuits saw these tracks." It was "not long – not many ou-yers (years) after seeing these tracks" that "Dr Rae & his party came again to this Bay but this last time they came in one boat." Nothing could be clearer or more factually correct. That Rae had come first with two boats and later with one was how the Inuit consistently discriminated between his two visits.[116] Eveeshuk's clear inference is that the tracks were seen between Rae's visits, a "long time" after the first but "not long" before the second. This ties in with Ouela's estimate that it was two years before Rae's return that these events transpired.

What emerges from Hall's rather involved methodology is a tendency to ascribe high dates (1855–64) when the Inuit were counting backwards through their own remembrances, but to ascribe earlier ones (1852–55) when referring to the visits by Rae. Karwonga, Artungun, Ouela, and Eveeshuk were certain that their encounters preceded Rae's return in 1854, while the tales using Kia as a reference seem to centre on the years 1855–56.

Rae's two expeditions (1846–47 and 1853–54) are the only certainly known and fixed points in this argument, and the fact that so many events are tied to the timeframe 1847–55 seems logically to imply that he was the source of the tales about Ekterlin. As we have seen, a partial case can be made for Rae as the inspiration of the Kia stories. But as he never approached Amitoke or Igloolik, he and his men cannot be used to explain the remembrances of Quasha, Artungun, or Armouyer.

Most historians find the Inuit chronology confusing and unconvincing. Rae, too, thought "this fitting in of dates" was "rather wonderful" and said he found it difficult to believe that "at the very time" he was at Repulse Bay, Crozier and one or two companions "were wandering about near us, killing abundance of deer, &c."[117]

Rae could not but be amazed at Hall's credulity in believing that Franklin's men could survive so long. He remarked, "It must be remembered that Crozier, if alive, could have had no inducement to live five or six years among the Esquimaux – as Hall's report, if true, would leave us to believe."[118] And he adamantly insisted that no survivors could have postdated his 1854 visit, remarking that "if Hall's story is to be believed, I and my companions must have been worse than fools"[119] to have missed them. Rae's point is well taken. It is possible, given the demonstrated reticence of Inuit hunters, that Rae was not told of all the encounters with strangers that occurred before his 1854 visit to the area. But it does seem improbable that he would not have heard about Etkerlin at nearby Koongwa only a few years before, though it should be remembered that at least some of the participants in these encounters had promptly "left I-wil-lik for Igloolik & did not see Dr Rae when at I-wil-lik last time."[120]

Rae was told of the fate of Franklin's starving men in 1854. Unfortunately, we cannot tell exactly what stories were current from the short consolidated statement that he preserved. But if white survivors were still alive between Repulse Bay and King William Island at that time, it does seem inconceivable that Rae would not have heard of them on his trip to the west that year.

Another interesting consideration is the Inuit reluctance to ascribe the various encounters to white men. Had they learned of the loss of many white men in their country, it would have been natural to conclude that these strangers were stragglers from Franklin's band. We can trace with some certainty how and when the news of the Franklin disaster spread among the native people. Some of Franklin's retreating men were seen by four hunters, one of whom was Hall's later informant Teekeeta. Teekeeta and his companions (with the possible exception of Tooshooarthariu) were all Netsilingmiut and lived most of the time near Willersted Lake on the southern Boothia Peninsula. Teekeeta's brother-in-law was the well-travelled Innookpoozhejook who gave Rae the first news of the Franklin disaster in 1854. Innookpoozhejook served as Hall's guide on his trip to King William Island fifteen years later, telling Hall that "before leaving Neitchille he saw Tut-ke-ta & his mother & had the story [of the Franklin disaster] from them."[121] He then went to Pelly Bay and told the stories to the Inuit there, who at that time "didn't know anything about the white men's starving."[122]

Innookpoozhejook's arrival at Pelly Bay can be accurately dated, for he attended a great meeting there of the various bands of Inuit the winter before Rae and his men came from the east (the winter of 1853–54). By this time, the western Inuit were sure that the last of Franklin's men were either dead or had reached their homes and that none remained in the Arctic.[123] The next year Rae found that the news of the Franklin disaster was widespread. He noted that he "offered large rewards in guns, knives, daggers, saws, &c., with still larger promises for the future if they could tell me of even one living white man. Their reply was always in the negative."[124] Also among those present at this congregation were Teekeeta's cousin Eekchooarchoo (Hall's "Jerry")[125] and a hunter named Aglooka. Both men were Igloolik natives, and they had presumably taken the tale of the Franklin survivors home to Igloolik by 1855 or 1856. Aglooka, who as a ten-year-old had been a favourite of Parry's crew at Igloolik, was also interviewed by Hall. He confirmed that Eekchooarchoo's mother (Teekeeta's aunt), who was "a Pelly Bay native," brought the news "about the white men starving near Neitchille" to the Repulse Bay natives.[126] Another participant re-called "hearing a great deal about the ships & Kob-lu-nas" when "Dr Rae & party passed through that part of the country."[127] Aglooka further related how he had been told by the same old lady of "a good many men together starving" and that "some started off from the main body of starving ones & never came back again. Every once in a while a part of the great many would go away & not return again."[128]

It thus becomes clear that until the winter before Rae's 1854 visit, the Inuit to the east of Boothia did not know about the Franklin disaster, and thus any strangers encountered would naturally have been thought to be Etkerlin. By the time of Hall's visit, knowledge of the Franklin tragedy had spread, and now second thoughts and doubts could emerge – as they almost invariably did – and the strangers were identified as white men. The point here is that the encounters took place and the tales were originally told before the possibility of white men entered into the picture – that is, before 1854.

Kia's tale is the pivot on which most of the Inuit relative chronology rests. Quasha and his wife saw the two white men at Nelikiok-big during the "same year"; Artungnun saw the dog the "same summer"; Armouyer discovered the *arnuk* the next year. Koolooa thought that his friend saw his stranger in 1854, but he must have been mistaken. Rae himself offered the crucial clue, for he recorded that "on my return to Repulse bay in 1853, the natives told me of [the Parry Bay] cairn ... and that three or four strangers (white men), or their footmarks, had been observed at the place or near it."[129] Kia told his friends at Igloolik of his encounter the following winter, and the news travelled to Repulse Bay in time for Rae to hear it in 1853. We must therefore conclude that Kia probably saw his white man in 1851 or 1852.[130]

The year after Kia's encounter there was some "trouble" at Igloolik, and the fact that Quasha's relative was murdered is frequently cited. Since Kia, the year before, had been worried about retribution for having killed another native, one might suspect that the "trouble" was related to a family feud that was being played out. On the other hand, Rae learned of "a terrible year of starvation and death" among the Repulse Bay Inuit, which had decimated their numbers in 1853.[131] Ik-ku-mer's wife thought that the presence of the strangers on the Melville Peninsula was the root cause of all the trouble.[132]

Hall originally, but unrealistically, had believed that the Melville Peninsula stories dated from 1860–64. As he continued his investigation, it became apparent that the stories all clustered within a few years of Rae's second expedition. Those dealing with Kia usually fell between 1854 and 1856, while those from Koongwa, Amitoke, and Repulse Bay were said to have been "before Dr Rae came back the second time." That the second variant is true is proved by the fact that Rae heard a version of Kia's story in 1853.

This could be seen as confirmation that Rae himself inspired the Koongwa tales and was Kia's man, all of these being remembrances of his first visit of 1847. But Rae never approached Amitoke or Nelikiokbig. If, on the other hand, these encounters are attributed to Parry, as is usually done, the Inuit timing is in error not by a few years but by two decades. So if we accept that white men were seen at these places in the early 1850s, we must, like Hall, conclude that they were survivors of the Franklin disaster.

This is in complete accord with the most detailed Inuit chronology – that of Ouela – that the strangers were seen "in the spring of the year & two years before Dr Rae & party came here the last time." If this is true, it would also explain Hall's firm and unshakeable belief that he was hearing about Franklin survivors. His editor Nourse and all subsequent historians have been perplexed by

Hall's fervour in defending this thesis even while he transcribed interviews that seemed to be at variance with it. Perhaps the answer is that only he was there, and only he heard the exact words of the Inuit and saw their faces as they told their stories. In spite of the apparent inconsistencies, many of which he probably created through poor translation and interview technique, Hall could tell that these people were speaking the truth.

The standard reconstruction of the Franklin disaster states that all the men died near King William Island in 1848, though this has recently been challenged.[133] If the accounts of strangers on the Melville Peninsula do in fact relate to the period between Rae's two visits, the conclusion seems inescapable. If white men were seen between Rae's two visits they must, by default, have come from Franklin's ships. So if we cannot convincingly ascribe the Etkerlin on Melville Peninsula to either Rae or Parry, we must investigate the only other possibility, however remote it may seem.

~*3*~

Homeward Bound

THE IWILLIK ALTERNATIVE

As discussed at length in an earlier book,[1] there is much evidence to suggest that more than one attempt was made by the members of the Franklin expedition to abandon their icebound ships in the hope of reaching safety. The failure of any of the party to succeed is usually explained as the result of ethnocentric blindness on the part of the commanding officers, in that they failed to learn lessons in survival from the Inuit, and the fact that they made a poor choice of route.

The Victory Point record of 1848 seems to give a clear indication of how Crozier expected to extricate his men. His addition of the meaningful postscript "and start tomorrow, 26th, for Backs Fish River" is seen as a statement that he intended to ascend that river with his whole company, presumably to reach Fort Providence, the Hudson's Bay Company outpost on Great Slave Lake. No certain relics of the marchers have been found farther south than Starvation Cove on the Adelaide Peninsula, which is still many miles north of the Great Fish River.

Modern commentators are universally shocked at Crozier's overestimation of the capabilities of his men. In 1834 it had taken George Back and his tiny party more than a month to ascend this turbulent river, which he described as "running through an iron-ribbed coun-

try without a single tree … and broken into falls, cascades, and rap-
ids, to the number of no less than eighty-three."[2] It seems incredible
that Crozier, who was undoubtedly familiar with Back's journey,
would not have realized that his party of 105 men faced an extremely arduous overland journey of more than 600 miles, most of it
through the aptly named Barren Lands, if they attempted this route.
When Back was asked by the Admiralty whether his river could be
used by the Franklin crews as a means of escape, he rejected "all and
every idea of any attempts on the part of Sir John Franklin to send
boats or detachments over the ice to any point of the mainland eastward of the Mackenzie River," because, as he explained, "I can say
from experience that no toilworn and exhausted party could have
the least chance of existence by going there."[3]

As a young lieutenant, Franklin had led an overland expedition
down the Coppermine River to the Arctic Ocean. During the return
journey through the Barren Lands, he had lost eleven of his twenty
men to starvation and exposure, the others surviving only with the
help of friendly Indians. Presumably Franklin, as overall commander, had confirmed Back's opinion and had indicated to Crozier that
any attempt to ascend the Great Fish River would be almost preor-
dained to failure.

The idea that this river was the intended retreat route is challenged by the testimony collected by Hall. In 1869 he interviewed
Teekeeta and Owwer, two of the four natives who actually met
Franklin survivors, and they were of the opinion that the leader of
this detachment, whom they called Aglooka, was not heading for
the Great Fish River. Teekeeta remembered that "Aglooka pointed
with his hand to the southward & eastward & at the same time repeating the word I-wil-lik. The Innuits could not understand
whether he wanted them to show him the way there or that he was
going there."[4] As we know, Iwillik was the Inuit name for a traditional campsite in Repulse Bay,[5] a fact that Franklin's officers
would have known from reading Parry's *Journal*.

As noted earlier, when Franklin died on 11 June 1847, overall
command of the expedition fell to Captain Crozier of the *Terror*. He
had served with Parry as a young midshipman at Winter Island
and Igloolik more than twenty years before and was therefore familiar with the eastern Inuit and the likelihood of meeting them at
Iwillik. By 1848, Crozier was one of the most experienced explorers
alive, having spent most of the intervening years involved in either

Arctic or Antarctic work. By contrast, most of the other officers of the Franklin expedition were young men with no experience in the ice.

Crozier was well known to the Inuit of the central Arctic, both under his own name, "Cro-zhar," and under his Inuit name, Aglooka.[6] Surprisingly, since the Inuit are traditionally thought not to have visited the two Franklin ships, the Pelly Bay natives remembered that the "same man, Crozier, who was at Igloolik when Parry and Lyon were there, was Esh-e-mu-ta ... of the two ships lost in the ice."[7] In most of the stories preserved by the Inuit concerning Franklin's men, the Eshemuta, or leader, is referred to as Aglooka, with the understanding that Crozier is being spoken of. The tradition that Crozier himself led his men and was one of the last to die was widespread. In fact, there is good reason to doubt whether Crozier survived to the last. But as commander and a man of experience, it is likely that his directives and opinions were taken into account when the final plans for retreat were made.

We have nothing to indicate Crozier's line of thought during this fateful time, apart from the cryptic eight words he had appended to Fitzjames's note. Yet he alone of the officers on the *Erebus* and *Terror* had lived among the Inuit at Igloolik. He knew that they often spent part of the year at Repulse Bay/Iwillik, and he must have realized that the best chance for his group lay in obtaining help from the natives. A careful study of the published narratives of earlier explorers would have shown Crozier a possible way to save his men. According to Thomas Simpson, who had travelled that way in 1839, the northern coast of Adelaide Peninsula along Simpson Strait provided good hunting for many Inuit.[8] Indeed, it remained prime hunting territory until this century. In 1833 Back had noticed a large native encampment near the mouth of the Great Fish River, an encampment that supported "about sixty or seventy" Inuit.[9]

From the Adelaide Peninsula, concentrations of Inuit lay like stepping-stones to the east. Sir John Ross met "about 160 souls"[10] during his three winters at Lord Mayor Bay, and more recent expeditions have confirmed that Pelly Bay remained an important Inuit centre. Rae encountered a hunting party of seventeen there in 1854, while Rasmussen counted fifty-four adults there in 1923.[11] Farther east, Committee Bay was also noted as a principal gathering place of the Inuit for seasonal hunting.[12]

Iwillik/Repulse Bay, the stated destination of Aglooka and his men, also held promise of native help. In 1821–22 Parry and Lyon had found "an immense Esquimaux settlement" there,[13] and this too has been more recently confirmed. On his arrival there in 1846, Rae found twenty-six individuals.[14] Hall spent the winter of 1865–66 at the nearby village of Nowyarn (Naujan) with forty-three Inuit,[15] and he noted one hundred and twenty-two (including twenty-six hunters) during the winter of 1868–69.[16] One hundred years later, Therkel Mathiassen described the "principal summer settlement" at Aivilik, which he said was the "most extensive Eskimo summer settlement I have ever seen."[17]

From Repulse Bay, another chain of traditional native encampments led to Igloolik. Parry and Lyon found "above sixty men, women, and children" at Winter Island,[18] and they encountered more in Lyon Inlet.[19] From researches conducted during this century, the anthropologist Franz Boas considered the latter place to have been "an important settlement,"[20] and the Inuit often told Hall of hunting in this region, known as Melokuta (or Mel-loo-kee-ta). Farther north, between Lyon Inlet and Igloolik, lived another group of related Inuit who spent much of their time at Ingnertoq (Ingnearing?), near Amitoke and South Ooglit Island. At the latter place, Hall found about one hundred natives in April 1868.[21]

Igloolik itself, which was very familiar to Crozier, was a major native centre. Parry reported about one hundred and fifty-five Inuit there in 1822[22] and considered it to be "one of their principal rendezvous, forming, as it were, a sort of central link in the very extensive chain of these peoples peregrinations."[23] When Hall visited in March 1867, he found a large village, counting forty-two women and many hunters. He noted that these natives "appeared to have frequent intercourse with Too-noo-nee (Pond's Bay)," which they could reach in only four days' travel.[24]

A short distance from Igloolik, Hall came across another village, which had twenty-three igloos.[25] When the first accurate attempts at a scientific census was undertaken, there were over five hundred Iglulik Inuit, who were divided almost equally between the Repulse Bay area, Igloolik, Pond Bay, and Admiralty Inlet (Baffin Island).[26] It was felt that there was "reason for believing the population [had] declined during the past few years."[27] This largely confirmed Parry's opinion of a century earlier, that "there may perhaps be three or four hundred people" living between Repulse Bay and Igloolik.[28]

The experts at home, heedful of the escape of the crew from Sir John Ross's icebound *Victory* in 1833, were aware that Franklin survivors might attempt to reach the whalers at Pond Bay, though it was generally felt that the men would proceed directly north along the eastern shore of the Boothia Peninsula as Ross's men had done. This route would have been slightly more direct than one through Repulse Bay but was not well populated with Inuit who could assist the survivors. Another factor favouring this route was the possibility of using the cache of food and boats left at Fury Beach by Parry in 1824, though if Crozier had read Ross's *Narrative* he would have known that Ross's men had pretty well exhausted this as a source of nourishment.[29] In any case, this cache at Fury Beach was rumoured to have been pillaged by Inuit or whalers.[30]

Rae favoured the Fury Beach alternative[31] and, not surprisingly, was convinced that Crozier would never have considered Repulse Bay or Igloolik as possible escape routes. Rae could "see no reason why any of Franklin's party should have wandered … in a direction the very opposite to that which we know by Esquimaux report the party took … by following which they would have fallen in with friendly Indians, who had been told to look out for them, and bring them in safety to the Hudson's Bay Company's settlements, which they would have done by traveling to the southwest for a shorter distance than 500 miles."[32] However, Rae's comment that the Iwillik alternative was "in a direction the very opposite to that which we know by Esquimaux report the party took" is contradicted by the evidence of Hall's informants. It presumably refers to the statement by Rae's informant that the last few men went south towards "Ook-koo-i-hi-ca-lik," which has consistently been read as the name for the mouth of the Great Fish River. This objection will be addressed shortly.

It is true that Repulse Bay is a long way from King William Island, but Rae misrepresents the distance to the Hudson's Bay Company settlements, the nearest of which, on Great Slave Lake, would have been even farther from the abandoned ships. In any case, this "settlement" was actually an isolated trading post, which would have offered little relief to a party of 105 men. Having himself travelled from Repulse Bay to King William Island, Hall could only regret that Crozier had not tried this eastern route. "We could have saved the whole company & brought them without the loss of a man back to Repulse Bay!" he asserted. "It is not with any egotistical feeling that

I say this but with a full confidence in what I now know of the country through wh. we have made this sledge journey." Hall's hunting records bear out his boast. The same day that he wrote the above, he and his native party killed twenty-one of the seventy or so musk-oxen they saw.[33] Their tally for the three-month return trip from Repulse to King William Land was seventy-nine musk-oxen, eighteen caribou, and two seals.[34] Hall commented:

What a pity that Crozier had not known the resources of the country from near King Williams Land thence to Repulse Bay by the route we have travelled to & from that Island for then he & Co. could have taken simply their sledges laden with guns & ammunition ... There could have been no difficulty in killing enough game to subsist the whole party provided Crozier had a few hunters like himself. And after getting to Repulse Bay, could Crozier & party have found no means of getting nearer the land of their homes, they could have lived for years on their own energetic efforts.[35]

The Inuit of Repulse Bay were not only closer and more accessible than the white traders at Great Slave Lake, but they were situated between two groups of white men, who were probably the hoped-for destination of the beleaguered crews. So if Crozier and his men had managed to reach Iwillik/Repulse Bay, there would have been two ways they could go. One would be a 250-mile journey north to Igloolik. The natives from there frequently visited Ponds Bay and Admiralty Inlet to hunt whales or to interact with British whalers. This fact, repeatedly referred to by Parry and Lyon, must have been well known to Crozier. This is the route the "Etkerlin" on the Melville Peninsula must have chosen if they were Franklin survivors. It would have been a good choice. In his study of the local Inuit, David Damas noted, "The Igluligmiut contacts with neighbours to the north (Pond Inlet and Admiralty Inlet Eskimo) and to the south (Repulse Bay people) were frequent ... During the nineteenth century, there seems to have been much travel between the areas of Pond Inlet, Repulse Bay, and Iglulik."[36]

It will be remembered that Armou and his father saw some Etkerlin while in the vicinity of Amitoke. It is interesting to note that Armou remembered that "these Indians [Etkerlin] attempted to reach that part of the North (near Pond's Bay) where Ar-mou's wife came from but they all starved & froze to death before getting there."[37] In 1882 Rae remarked that "a story has been told, coming

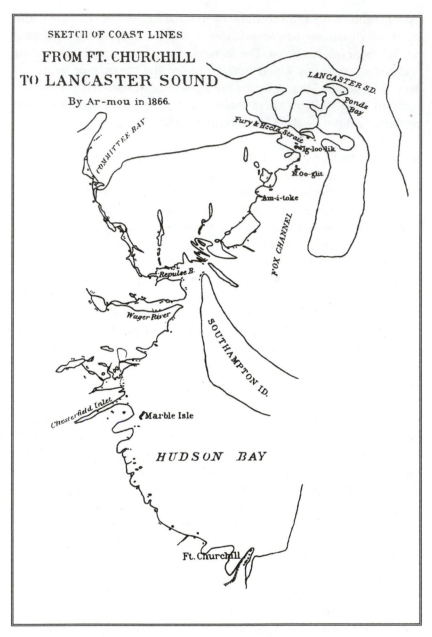

SKETCH OF COAST LINES
FROM FT. CHURCHILL
TO LANCASTER SOUND
By Ar-mou in 1866.

This map, drawn by Armou, shows the Inuit familiarity with the coast from
Churchill to Ponds Bay. (Smithsonian Institution)

from some whalers, who visited Pond's Bay near 600 miles north-east of the scene of the sad disaster, that Franklin's people had been murdered by the Eskimos."[38] Of course, Rae did not believe it.

The second possibility for any Franklin survivors who reached Iwillik would be to travel 500 miles south towards the Hudson's Bay Company post at Fort Churchill. There was a chain of traditional In-uit encampments leading south, including those at Depot Island, Cape Fullerton, and Nuvuk (Hall's "Noowook") south of Wager Bay.[39] Annual supply ships from England called at Fort Churchill and at the much larger settlement of York Factory. The latter, 200 miles south of Churchill, was a fair-sized town.[40] The fur trader R.M. Ballantyne, who visited York Factory a few years before Fran-klin's departure from England, indicated that between thirty and forty white men were perpetually stationed there and that it served as the main depot for the Hudson's Bay Company, stocked with "two year's outfit for the whole northern department."[41] If the Fran-klin crews had been able to reach either of these places, their chances of rescue would have been excellent.

However, because of the presence of the fierce Caribou Inuit and Indians to the south, it is unlikely that Inuit at Repulse Bay would have directed white survivors in that direction. Birket-Smith felt that the natives of Repulse and Pelly bays may have occasionally visited Chesterfield Inlet but that "if Eskimos have ever come from ... Re-pulse Bay to Marble Island other than women who may have mar-ried into the tribes of the Caribou Eskimos, it must be said to have been accidentally."[42] The Repulse Bay Inuit themselves rarely trav-elled so far south, though sporadic individual contact did occur.[43] The Caribou Inuit farther south "had already accustomed them-selves to visiting Churchill regularly, where they bought knives, ar-row and spear heads and old nails."[44] On the other hand, the Netsilingmiut of Pelly Bay frequently made use of an inland route to trade to the south.

The travels of Rae and Hall prove that such long journeys were possible, though it should be remembered that neither was encum-bered with one hundred companions. In 1854 Rae travelled from Repulse Bay to the Castor and Pollux River and returned in fifty-seven days. Hall, following the same route, reached King William Island forty-seven days after leaving Repulse, his slower rate of travel being a consequence of relying on Inuit guides who were in no particular hurry. Hall's entire return trip to King William Island took ninety days, while his visit to Melville Peninsula, including side trips to Parry Bay and Gifford Fiord, and days spent at Ooglit and Igloolik interviewing natives, took just ninety-two.

In the last years of the nineteenth century, missionaries and explorers opened the Barren Lands with remarkable journeys,[45] and travellers during the twentieth century confirmed that such long trips were possible, even by solitary white men. David Irwin walked, usually alone, across the entire Canadian Arctic in the 1930s.[46] A missionary named Jack Turner, travelled unaccompanied from Pond Bay to King William Island (by the roundabout way of Igloolik, Ross Bay, and Pelly Bay) in the early 1940s.[47] Yet one must not lose sight of the fact that speculation concerning an eastern detachment of Franklin's men is completely unproven. Except for the stories collected by Hall and an enigmatic reference to "Iwillik" by the white leader of the Franklin men seen on King William Island, there is no real evidence to support the theory that any Franklin survivors proceeded in the direction of the Melville Peninsula, regardless of how logical such an attempt might be.

What is needed is a "bridge" of some kind – indications of strangers in the intervening lands and relics of their passage. As the survivors would have been few in number, they would have left only the faintest traces; and as they would have passed over the same ground explored by Rae in 1854, it is probable that signs of their passing would have been confused with his. As before, only the Inuit testimony holds the promise of separating the various threads.

A FOOL'S ERRAND

Ten years after Hall's return to the United States, another American expedition came to the Arctic to investigate stories of strange white men – presumed survivors of Franklin's expedition. A cavalry lieutenant, Frederick Schwatka, and his second-in-command, the journalist William Gilder, had been enticed to the North by stories told by the American whalers who had taken over the "fishery" in Hudson Bay. In particular, they had been inspired by the story of Captain Barry.

Barry told of a visit that a family of Inuit made to his whaler, the *Glacier*, which had been frozen in at Repulse Bay between 1871 and 1873. These Inuit "spoke of a stranger in uniform who had visited them some years before, and who was accompanied by many other white men." According to Barry, the natives asserted that all the white men had afterwards died, "but the chief [white man] meanwhile collected a great quantity of papers. He had left these papers behind him in a cairn, where, among other things, some silver spoons had since been found."[48] Nor was this the only time Barry heard of strange white men. In the winter of 1876, while serving in the *A. Houghton* at Marble Island, Barry met another group of Inuit, who "while looking at his logbook said that the great white man who had been among them many years before had kept a similar book, and having told him this one of them gave him a spoon engraved with the word 'Franklin.' "[49]

Barry's stories were treated with a healthy amount of scepticism by the experts at home, even though Tookoolitoo's husband Ebierbing, who was now working as an interpreter for the Americans, "declared the story was a fact."[50] In view of what was then known about the fate of Franklin's men, it seemed impossible that any survivors could have reached Repulse Bay. There was also considerable confusion about the location of the supposed cairn that the "stranger in uniform" had built. Barry said it was "reported to be located on an island in the Gulf of Boothia," a probable reference to the large island at the southern terminus of Committee Bay which Rae had named for the Prince of Wales (now simply Wales Island). Interestingly, this island had the same Inuit name as the site of the Franklin wreck: Shartoo.[51]

Barry's tale was well publicized in the American press, and some version of it was forwarded to the British Admiralty for evaluation. The Admiralty in turn sent the information to John Rae, and from his response we obtain a more precise location for the supposed cairn as "a place on the Arctic coast, about thirty miles south of Cape Inglefield [i.e., Englefield]."[52] This confirms that Barry's cairn was either the monument found by Hall in Parry Bay or the hidden cache nearby.

Schwatka's journal, which has only recently been discovered and published, confirms that Barry's tale was focused on the northwestern shore of the Melville Peninsula. He remarked that Barry "had placed the position of the Franklin cairn – the very goal which brought us here – either on Cape Englefield (on the Melville Peninsula) or on King William Land" and noted that "an examination of the map will show these localities to be so far apart as to make it im-

possible for a single expedition to thoroughly explore both."[53]
Schwatka thus decided to confine his efforts to King William Island.
Predictably, Rae cast scorn on Barry and his Inuit testimony. He
concluded, "The whole report ... I believe to be a mistake in all its
important particulars, and if the Franklin records are ever found, it
certainly will not be anywhere in the neighborhood of Cape Inglefield."[54]

The stories told by Captain Barry had two apparently contradictory threads. One concerned Franklin survivors and artifacts, particularly a collection of papers. The other dealt with a cairn on the
Melville Peninsula near Parry Bay. It should be pointed out that
Hall's edited *Narrative* of his sojourn was not published until 1879,
six years after Barry recorded the above events. Nevertheless, the
whalers, having supported Hall and given him passage in their vessels, were undoubtedly familiar with his main findings. We should
perhaps not be surprised that Barry's tales have echoes in the similar
stories told to Hall by Kia, Koolooa, and Artungun. They therefore
lose some of their force as corroboration, and the consensus has generally been that either Captain Barry had misunderstood what he
had been told or that the Inuit themselves had been confused.

When the members of the Schwatka expedition arrived at Repulse Bay in 1879, they immediately began to make inquiries about
Captain Barry's stories. Unfortunately, they soon learned that one
of the principal Inuit informants had died and "that nobody knew
what had become of the other."[55] Yet this still left the corroborative
Franklin spoon to be investigated:

Nutargeark ... said he had brought a spoon with him from King William
Land, which corresponded in description with the one Barry took to the
United States. He said it was given to him by some of his tribe, and that it
had come from one of the boat places, or where skeletons had been found
on King William Land or Adelaide Peninsula, he could not remember exactly where. He had not given the spoon to Captain Barry, but to the wife
of Sinuksook, an Iwillik Esquimau, who afterward gave it to Captain Potter. We saw Sinuksook's wife a little later, and she distinctly remembered
having given the spoon to Captain Potter. It was necessary, therefore, to
find this officer.[56]

The discovery that the famous spoon had come from King William
Island rather than from some "imaginary" cairn on Melville Pen-

insula ensured that Schwatka and Gilder would direct their search to the west. Even more damning to Barry's credibility was the suggestion that he had in fact stolen the spoon from Captain Potter. On locating the captain, Gilder questioned him closely:

I asked him [Captain Potter] if he remembered Captain Barry's getting a Franklin spoon while with him on the GLACIER, and he said he had never heard anything about it until he read in the newspapers that Barry had sent one to Sir John Franklin's niece, Miss Craycroft [Cracroft], which surprised him very much. He further said that he (Potter) had received three spoons at that time, one of which mysteriously disappeared shortly afterward. The published description of Barry's spoon corresponded exactly with the one he had lost, even to its being broken off near the bowl and mended with copper, as was the one he had received from Sinuksook's wife. Captain Potter further said, that to one who had lived with the Esquimaux, and acquired the pigeon [pidgin] English they use in communicating with the whalers in Hudson's Bay, and contrasted it with the language they use in conversation with each other, the assertion of Captain Barry, that he overheard them talking about books and understood them, was supremely ridiculous.

In this crucible of fact the famous spoon melted. So far as Captain Barry and his clews [clues] were concerned, we had come on a fool's errand.[57]

The stories collected by Barry from his native informants have eluded us. Nevertheless, there are faint and compelling echoes of the stories Hall had collected earlier. The linkage of two distant and supposedly unrelated locations in the central Arctic, the strange white man "in uniform" who led his men ("all of whom had afterward died") east to Repulse Bay, the buried records near a cairn on the northwestern shore of Melville Peninsula – all these are elements that have clear counterparts in the tales of Kia and Koolooa.

CONFLICTING TALES

In 1854 a native named Imike-pa-hu-gi-uke told Rae of an encounter between some Inuit and about forty survivors of the fateful Franklin march. Hall also interviewed this man, who was known to him as Innook-poo-zhe-jook, and learned the names of the four hunters who had actually seen Franklin's men. Owwer, Teekeeta, Mangaq, and Tooshooarthariu had taken their families to King William Island and had come across some white men dragging a boat on a sled along the shore of Washington Bay. As mentioned above, Hall managed to interview the first two of these men in 1869. Their stories were consistent, adding much more detail to what was known of the encounter. They convincingly confirmed and corroborated the account given second-hand to Rae many years before.[58]

As Teekeeta and Owwer told Hall, they and their families had camped with the white men for an indeterminate period (not exceeding a few days) and then abandoned them to their fate. This was later confirmed by Tooshooarthariu's wife Ahlangyah, who told Schwatka of the same encounter in 1879. Mangaq's son also recalled the incident when interviewed by Rasmussen in 1923.[59] We give the account as it was related to Hall:

Teekeeta and Owwer now tell that they with Tooshooarthariu and Mangaq ... they began to see many black objects moving along with what they had first espied as white in the distance. The object that they 1st had seen as white proved to be a sail raised on the boat ... the party with the boat and one other sledge passed by going a little lower down to a point or cape of the little bay where they then were ... Tooshooarthariu and Owwer started to meet them, walking there on the ice ... After each man Innuit had given ... some seal meat, it was all put on a (one) dog's back & then by the request of Aglooka [the white leader] all 4 Innuit men with the dog laden with meat went down with Aglooka and the man with him to where the men and the boat were, the men erecting a tent ... After tent of white men was all in complete order for sleeping in it, Aglooka went with the Innuits to their tents, which the women had erected while their husbands were absent with Aglooka.[60]

Tooshooarthariu himself was never interviewed by a white explorer, but his mother confirmed the details of this meeting on King William Island.[61] When Hall learned the details in 1869 he felt disillusioned. Having been inspired in his quest by a belief in Franklin survivors, and encouraged by the stories of strange white men wandering on the Melville Peninsula, he was shattered to learn that the Inuit had "heartlessly" abandoned the scurvy-ridden heroes. He wrote: "I am of the undoubted opinion that Innuits in general would let white men starve at their very doors if they had not the idea that by saving them they would be rewarded in something that they wanted," and he said he was sure that "if any of Sir John Franklin's men were ever seen by any of that people on Melville Peninsula, they were shunned thinking that the unfortunate creatures would be a tax upon their own stuffed but never satisfied stomachs."[62]

Although Hall had previously accepted every Inuit pronouncement at face value and had often remarked in his notes about these people's prodigious memories and amazing recall of facts, he now decided that most Inuit testimony was a fabric of lies on which little reliance could be placed. This attitude was probably largely due to the fact that soon after his arrival in the Arctic he had heard another version of Tooshooarthariu's meeting with the white men, a story that had been much more in tune with Hall's own dreams and ambitions.

Almost immediately on his arrival at Repulse Bay, Hall had been told that the Inuit were familiar with the story of the white men who had died farther west. But he had been overjoyed to learn from them that "four souls of Sir John Franklin's Expedition" had been heard from, and he had exulted: – "One of these F.R.M. Crozier! Three of these may yet be alive. The Innuits think they are."[63] Hall explained how he had come by this information: "By help of Jerry [Eek-choo-ar-choo] & Pa-pa in answer to my question if all the white men died who were a long time ago at Ki-ki-tung as he told me he [Kobbig] said 'All but 2 & one of them Ag-loo-ka.' These 2 men seen by three natives of his (Kob-big's) acquaintance, one Too-shoo-art-thar-u, another [blank] & the 3d [blank]. The last seen of them they went south."[64] Hall's principal informants in this matter were Ouela and his brothers:

This morning I have had another talk with Ou-e-la, Shoo-she-ark-nuk & Ar-too-a about some of the men of Franklin's Expedition. The man who caught seals for Eg-loo-ka (Crozier) & his men – the three with him (C.) – is their cousin. His name Too-shoo-art-thar-ri-u. He has another name which is *Kar-noo-e-nu-un* & is the son of old Ook-bar-loo's sister ... Too-shoo-art-thar-ri-u is same age as See-gar who is an inhabitant of our Igloo village. Both were boys about 10 years of age when Parry was at Igloolik. Too-shoo-art-tar-ri-u told them (Ou-e-la, Shoo-she-ark-nuk, Ar-too-a & Nuk-er-zhu) all about Crozier, the two ships & of the men's starving etc. etc. when they were stopping at Ok-kee-bee-jee-loo-a (Pelly Bay). It was the same year when the few Kob-lu-nas came there having with them an Innuit whose name was Oo-ling-buck. (This of course refers to Dr Rae & his men & therefore the time was 1854. All the brothers named saw Dr Rae in 1847 & also in 1854). They (the Innuits with whom I had the interview) counted with fingers the number of years ago when at Pelly Bay & made 10 & maybe one more. When their cousin, Too-shoo-art-tar-ri-u, 1st found Crozier & the three men with him, Crozier's face looked bad – his eyes all sunk in – looked so bad that their cousin could not bear to look at his face. Their cousin gave Crozier a bit of raw seal as quick as he could when he 1st saw him – Did not give any to the other three for they were fat & had been eating the flesh of their companions. It was near Neitch-il-le that this occured [sic] on the ice. Their cousin is now living at Neitchille. When he (Too-shoo-art-tar-ri-u) 1st saw Crozier & the men with him he was moving, having a loaded sledge drawn by dogs. He was going from place to place – making Igloos on the ice – & sealing – he had with him his wife, whose name is *Eelaing-nur* [Schwatka's "Ahlangyah"] & children. Crozier & his men had guns & a plenty of powder shot & ball. The Cousin took Crozier & his men along with him & fed them & took good care of them all winter. – Bye & bye they all moved to Neitchille & lived with the Innuits who are very numerous there. One of the men who was with Crozier died – not because he was hungry but because he was sick. Beside a high cliff Innuits saw something like Now-yers (Gulls) fall down to the ground dead & would not touch them for Crozier had done something to them – they (the Innuits) knew not what. In the summer Crozier & his men killed with their guns a great many birds – ducks, geese & Rein-deer. Crozier killed many – very many of the latter. The Innuits saw him do it. A Neitch-il-le Innuit went with Crozier & his remaining two men when they started to go to their country. They had a Ki-ak with which to cross rivers & lakes. They went down toward *Oot-koo-seek-ka-lik* (the Estuary of Great Fish or Back's river). Their cousin liked Crozier very much. Crozier wanted to give their cousin his gun but he would not accept it for he (the cousin) was afraid of it – he did not know any thing about how to use it. Crozier gave him his long knife (*sword* as Too-koo-li-too & E-bier-bing interpret it) & nearly every thing he had. He (C.) had many pretty things. Crozier told Too-shoo-art-tar-ri-u all about what had happened but he (T.) could not understand all.[65]

Two years after learning the above, Hall interviewed Kiutuk and was initially disappointed to hear that she had "never heard of any white men or man living along with Innuits." However, with her next sentence she confirmed that "all she knows is that Too-shoo-art-thar-u saw Ag-loo-ka & some men took them home & made them well." When asked if she herself had ever seen Tooshooarthariu, she confided that "he is all the same as father to me. Have heard him tell all about Ag-loo-ka. Ag-loo-ka was very sick, poor & hungry & Too-shoo-art-thar-u took him home fed him on salmon & seal & he got fat & well again. Too-shoo-art-thar-u did never tell her much about Ag-loo-ka but she has often heard him telling stories about him to other older Innuits."[66]

When Hall interviewed Tooshooarthariu's aunt Ookbarloo, he learned that "Aglooka and his three men" had lived "on the ice in an igloo with her nephew" and that "one man would not eat the flesh of his frozen and starved companions."[67] Old Ookbarloo confirmed and elaborated on the testimony of her sons. She said that her nephew Tooshooarthariu had rescued four white men and that one of them had subsequently died "for he was very sick. He did not die from hunger, but because he was very sick."[68] Neither Ouela nor Ookbarloo specifically dated the encounter between Tooshooarthariu and the white men. But it must have been before 1854, for they met Tooshooarthariu at Pelly Bay in that year and heard his stories. At that time, "the cousin had not heard whether Crozier [Aglooka] and the two men and Neitchille Innuit had ever come back or not."[69]

Ookbarloo noted that at the time of the encounter with the white men, Tooshooarthariu and his wife "had but one child ... though the wife had another prospective one – a little one in her (in utero) 'about as big as her fist.'"[70] After much effort and uncertainty, Hall determined that when the Inuit had congregated at Pelly Bay in 1854, that infant had attained "the size & age as either of the three little children" who were at present in Hall's igloo. These children ranged from "a little over four years old" to about six.[71] This would place the encounter with the white men between 1848 and 1850, precisely the timeframe for Franklin's men to have been trying to escape their detention.

The two Tooshooarthariu stories seem irreconcilable, as Hall realized. In the first scenario, described by his hunting companions Owwer and Teekeeta, Tooshooarthariu meets forty men on King William Island, spends a few days with them, and departs. The white men do little if any hunting, they carry their equipment on sleds, and their bodies are found the next year. This tale was corroborated not only by Tooshooarthariu's friends but by his wife. In the second story, told by Tooshooarthariu's aunt and cousins, he meets four white men on the ice, nurses them through a winter (except one who died of a sickness), and sends them on their way with a native guide. The leader of the white men, named Aglooka, hunts proficiently. The men apparently carry their equipment on their shoulders.

There are some similarities between the two accounts. In both, Tooshooarthariu was accompanied by his wife, and in both he offered the white men a small piece of seal meat on their first meeting. We might suspect that Tooshooarthariu had seen two different parties of white men, but the testimony of his wife Ahlangyah made no mention of a later encounter; she specifically stated that Schwatka was the first living white man she had seen since the encounter on King William Island.[72] Teekeeta also confirmed that his friend Tooshooarthariu "never saw Aglooka after [that] time."[73]

The discordant elements of the second tale could easily be ignored as exaggeration or fabrication except for one thing. They apparently have independent corroboration. In 1881 Captain W. Adams of the *Arctic* was whaling in Prince Regent Inlet in the vicinity of Fury and Hecla Strait when he received aboard a young Inuit hunter. This young man had a very interesting tale to tell:

The native stated that when he was a young man in his father's hut three men came over the land towards Repulse Bay and that one of them was a great Captain. The other two lived some little time in his father's hut, and he showed Captain Adams the spot on the chart where they were buried. The Esquimaux, continuing his narrative, said that seventeen persons started from two vessels which had been lost far to the westward but only three were able to survive the journey to his father's hut ... Assuming that what the Esquimaux stated was correct it would seem that the members of the Franklin expedition were attempting to reach Hudson Bay Territory. Judging from the present age of the native, Captain Adams is of the opinion that his allusion to having seen the men when he was a young man must refer to a period some thirty five years ago.[74]

Captain Adams's informant seems to have been the son of the Tooshooarthariu who nursed the survivors through the winter. It is interesting that he said that "three men came over the land towards Repulse Bay and that one of them was a great Captain." This is reminiscent of Captain Barry's "stranger in uniform," also a great Captain, "who was accompanied by many other white men," all of whom subsequently died.

Hall was totally perplexed by these conflicting tales. Perhaps there were two natives named Tooshoorthariu, for Inuit adults had many names and often shared the same name (Parry met no less than four natives named Toolooak between 1821 and 1823).[75] Perhaps Ouela and his brothers had two cousins who met Franklin survivors, and when Hall was told their various stories he mixed them together and assigned the name of one cousin to both versions. Interestingly, Hall wrote that Ouela's cousin "has two names," the second one being Kar-noo-e-nu-un. In fact, Ahlangyah's husband appears under a third name, Qablut, in another version of the encounter at King William Island.[76]

Was Hall hearing two different stories of encounters with white men? Did he meld them into discordant stories under the name of Tooshoorthariu? The details of the two traditions deserve closer scrutiny.

TWO AGLOOKAS

Two different traditions exist about a meeting between white men and an Inuit nephew of Ookbarloo. Each tradition has independent corroboration. The testimony of Captains Adams and Barry support that told by Ookbarloo, Ouela, Shookshearknuk, and Artooa, while Owwer and Teekeeta's version is supported by no less an authority than Tooshoorthariu's wife Ahlangyah. There are certain similarities between the two versions, but there are also disturbing discrepancies.

Perhaps the greatest divergence is in the reported amount of time spent with the white men. Teekeeta and Owwer stated that they spent one day and one night with Aglooka, leaving him and his companions in the morning – though their evasive answers caused Hall to conclude that "these Innuits feel guilty of letting white men starve & thus their inconsistent stories. They deviate as no truth telling men."[77] Tooshoorthariu's wife Ahlangyah told Schwatka that she and her party had remained with the white men for five days.[78] Tooshoorthariu's mother confirmed that "they [the white men] were all so hungry & poor that they (the Innuits) *all got up & ran away from them in the night while they were asleep.*" When asked how long her son spent with Aglooka, she replied, "Saw them only one day or part of one day for when night came the Innuits all left them."[79] In this variant of the Tooshoorthariu story, the time spent was short – at most a matter of a few days – and it cannot be reconciled with the account which states that Tooshooarthariu cared for the men "all winter."

Another discrepancy is the season. Teekeeta, Owwer, and Ahlangyah all offered graphic evidence that the summer was well advanced and that the ice was about to break up near King William Island: "late in the spring – in July … the sea ice nearly ready to break up. The ice full of holes every where about there – snow had all disappeared on the land. The sun had stopped in its course upward – was in sight all the time – ice in some of the lakes had dissolved – Ducks, gulls Nowyers etc. all in abundance in the various pools, ponds & lakes."[80] Yet according to Ookbarloo, "it was in the spring of the year though then very cold weather when her nephew found Eg-loo-ka [Aglooka] & the three men with him. It was a long time before the sea ice went away."[81] Confirming that her nephew cared for the white men for an extended period, she remarked that "it was in the fall of the year, in warm weather," when they started for their own land.[82]

One curious feature of both stories is the supposed destination of Aglooka and his men. Seegar had indicated that, on leaving Tooshooarthariu's care, Aglooka and his companions had gone south towards Ootkooseekalik (Utkuhigjalik). Hall interpreted this place name as "the Estuary of Great Fish or Back's river," and this agrees with the Victory Point record, which pointed to "Back's Great Fish River" as the direction (if not the destination) of Crozier's intended march. Rae had similarly heard that white men's remains had been found near the estuary of this river, which the natives called Ook-koo-i-hi-ca-lik. Although Teekeeta and Owwer said that Aglooka indicated that Iwillik was his destination and although they did not mention Ootkooseekalik, Hall nevertheless assumed that this was where Aglooka, his two companions, and his guide were bound.

Ouela and his brothers also said that Aglooka and his three men "went down toward Oot-koo-seek-ka-lik." However, their mother, old Ookbarloo, vehemently disagreed. She was very specific: "They went on the land to the southward. Eg-loo-ka said they were going to that part of the country (as the old lady described it – that part of the country occupied by the Innuits to the south of our present winter Quarters) belonging to the Kin-na-pa-toos. Too-koo-li-too says: 'I (T.) think from what the old lady has said, that Crozier & his few men with him, was going to try & get where the Kob-lu-nas live – either to Fort Churchill or York Factory.' "[83]

Kobbig also remarked that "the last seen" of Aglooka and his final companions "they went south." Ootkooseekalik, in its role as the Great Fish River, is southwest of Pelly Bay (where the Inuit implied Tooshooarthariu spent the winter with his guests) and is even farther southwest of Repulse Bay. Even taking into account the imprecise nature of Inuit geography, there is no way one can reconcile the Great Fish River with Ookbarloo's description of "south of our present winter Quarters" at Repulse Bay. As Ookbarloo indicated, both Churchill and York Factory were along the coast to the south.

The answer to this seeming discrepancy lies in the Inuit propensity to use identical descriptive names to identify widely separated geographical points. For, as Parry noted, Wager River (modern Wager Bay) was called Ootkooseek-salik. Parry further remarked that "the Esquimaux gave us information of an arm of the sea lying opposite to Wager River, on the Northern Coast of America, which they also distinguish by the same name, and which is only one or two days' journey distant from the other."[84] Here not only is confirmation that the Back (Great Fish) River estuary and Wager Bay shared the same name, but it provides the interesting detail that they afforded a short cut from the area of Neitchille to the coast of Hudson Bay.[85] Anyone travelling to Churchill or York Factory from Pelly Bay or Repulse Bay would have had to pass through the country of the "Kinnapatoo" Inuit. These were the Qairnirmiut Inuit who lived near Baker Lake and hunted near Chesterfield Inlet, which lies directly to the south of Wager Bay.

Another dissimilarity between the two tales of Tooshooarthariu concerns the white men's boat. In the King William Island tradition, the boat is a standard whaleboat, drawn on a sled, in which many of the white men slept. The "ki-ak" used by Aglooka and his three men was quite different. The white men "had a small boat that had places on the sides that would hold wind (air) … There were sticks or poles for this Boat to keep it open (spread) when used. This small Boat was wrapt or rolled up in a bundle or pack & carried on the shoulder of one of the men. The sides of this Boat something like Innuit's drugs [inflatable seal skins or bladders] that could be filled with air."[86]

Hall was convinced that he was hearing of an inflatable "India-rubber" boat and concluded that "Franklin may have had in his vessels a Boat or Boats called Halkett's air-Boat or its equivalent." Franklin did in fact have the recently invented Halkett boats aboard his vessels. Unfortunately for our purposes, so did Rae, though he makes no mention of having taken one on any of his journeys away from Repulse Bay. The Iwillik Inuit remembered "that when Dr Rae was here the 1st time he had an India Rubber boat wh. was blown away by a Nor Western & lost but this was found again on Dr. R's return from his spring journies in 1847."[87] We do not know whether Rae took his inflatable boat on his 1854 trek to Castor and Pollux River, but we do know that on that trip all of their equipment was carried on sleds.[88]

The behaviour of the white men in the two Tooshooarthariu tales is also at variance. In Teekeeta and Owwer's version, the men were hungry. They fished for salmon and killed birds, but they also traded for seal meat and fish. The Inuit abandoned them "and their remains were found the next year." Although the hunters disingenuously remarked that they did not know that the white men were starving, their description of the men belies this. In the other version, Ookbarloo and her sons told how Aglooka "learned as fast as he could how to kill Took-too (rein-deer) ducks, geese, gulls, etc."[89] She told how, in her nephew's care, Aglooka grew "very well & fat" and how his men "all lived & grew fat." The surviving white men had learned the lessons of survival so well from their Inuit hosts that the natives told Hall they were sure Aglooka and his companions "are alive yet – think that they may have returned to Neitch-il-le if they found they could not get home to the Kob-lu-na country, & lived again with Innuits."[90]

It will be remembered that in the story told by Captain Barry, the "stranger in uniform ... collected a great quantity of papers." The Inuit remembered that he had "left these papers behind him in a cairn" and that "the great white man who had been among them many years before had kept a similar book" to Barry's logbook. Captain Adams reportedly returned to England with "a few papers found in the vicinity of the Fury and Hecla Straits."[91] (I have not been able to locate these papers in any archive, so presumably they were unilluminating.) Tooshooarthariu's sister also remembered that the white leader Aglooka "gave to her brother a large package of papers" and that "he told him a great deal about what to do with it but Too-shoo-art-thar-i-u couldn't comprehend what Ag-loo-ka meant."[92]

Tooshooarthariu's mother also remembered that her son had very many papers and books but thought that they came from the places where Ross had wintered his *Victory* in the 1830s.[93] These papers were distributed among the Pelly Bay natives. Most of them were given to the children as playthings. In March 1866 Hall interviewed Ouela's wife, who had joined the other Repulse Bay Inuit when they were at Pelly Bay in 1854, and she remembered that "a woman by the name of I-see-wont … gave a paper having writing on it" to her mother.[94] The paper was "long & narrow" (Hall indicates a size of 12 by 5 inches) and was "written only one side … the paper not torn a bit."[95] Unfortunately, this piece of paper was thrown away "only two days before she saw Dr Rae in 1854 at this place."[96]

Tooshooarthariu's sister confirmed that many of these papers had survived until quite recently, Hall noted, and that "many of these were in the possession of Innuits at Pelly Bay when Dr Rae was there last time"; but "neither he or Mar-ko [Rae's interpreter] ever asked for anything of the kind. Now she is very sorry her brother did not keep them till he saw some one who wanted such things."[97] Kobbig's brother had been one of the last to possess a manuscript paper, which Tooshooarthariu "had a long time before given him."[98] Hall's disappointment was complete when he learned that this relic too had only recently been destroyed.

When Hall later met Tooshooarthariu's companions Owwer and Teekeeta near King William Island, he asked them about the papers given to their friend by Aglooka. Having seen little similarity between the two sets of Tooshooarthariu stories, it is not particularly surprising that their memory of the facts varied from that of the Repulse Bay natives in this respect too. They told Hall that "Aglooka to their knowledge never gave Tooshooarthariu any papers or package."[99]

OOLIZHAR AND OOLIZE

An important element of Inuit testimony is the preservation of names. To lend verisimilitude to their accounts, many of the natives gave lists of Inuit who were involved or who could corroborate what was being said. They delighted in learning the names of any strangers and preserved them with remarkable accuracy for generations.

Throughout his notes and journals, Hall continually substituted "Crozier" for the Inuit name for the chief white survivor in Tooshooarthariu's care. He felt justified in doing this even though the Inuit rarely referred directly to "Cro-zhar" but repeatedly used two different names for the leader, Aglooka (which Hall sometimes spelled "Eglooka") and Oolizhar. Aglooka (roughly translated as "strider") was a common Inuit name often given to tall white men, who always seemed to be hurrying about purposefully. It is true that this was also Crozier's Inuit name, which he had gained by the method of name transference with a popular ten-year-old boy at Igloolik in 1822–23.[100] But Aglooka was so common a name for white officers that it loses most of its value as identification. For example, it was also given to Parry, Rae, and James Clark Ross (the nephew of Sir John Ross).

Knowing that other white explorers had shared the Inuit nickname Aglooka, Hall persevered in trying to discover the "kobluna name" of the white leader. Shooshuarknuk told him that the man Tooshooarthariu rescued was called Oo-li-zharn,[101] and Koongeouelik confirmed that he "heard Too-shoo-art-thar-i-u his cousin tell him of *Ag-loo-ka* (Oo-li-zen)."[102] Hall, perhaps influenced by his own preconceptions, assured his readers that this "is really the way old Ouk-bar-loo generally pronounces the name Crozier."[103] Having asked Erktua to pronounce Crozier, he reported: "She responded 'Oo-li-zhar' & this was as near as she could pronounce Crozier. I may here say that some Innuits can speak the name 'Crozier' quite distinctly after many trials, but leave them alone awhile & they, among themselves, almost without exception, speak it Oo-li-zhar."[104] To emphasize how the "kobluna names" of white men often posed problems for the Inuit (as indeed did native names for the white men), Hall explained: "I will give a few instances of the peculiar pronunciation the Innuits give to names they have heard spoken: Chapel they speak See-pee-lar. Ask them to speak the name Chapel after you, 'See-pee-lar' will be the result of their best efforts. Ask them to say Mr Binks: Mr Bin. Chester they speak She-a-ter – Hall they pronounce Hull & occasionally one gets it *Hell* & perhaps all would speak it same way if they really knew what a *hot* place it represents."[105]

Some Inuit apparently had a better ear for white men's names than others did. When Hall asked Erktua the names of the white men she could remember meeting at Igloolik when she was a young girl, he had quite good results:

I began by asking Erk-tu-a to repeat to me all the names she could recollect of the Kob-lu-nas she saw when at Ig-loo-lik. She began & continued thus:

Par-ee – he Esh-e-mut-ta (Captain)

Ly-on – he Esh-e-mut-ta (Captain)

Par-me – he Esh-e-mut-ta-nar (Mate on Lyon's ship)

Oo-li-ze – on Parry's ship

Cro-zhar – Esh-e-mut-ta-nar (Mate or some officer not so great as Captain on Parry's ship)

Pe-zart – a tall man who she thinks was on Lyon's ship

Marg – steward of Parry's ship – same name as Parry's *an-ma-ma* (mother) a boy on Lyon's ship same name

Hend-son – she remembered well – a jolly fellow would swing his arms & cry *An-ne-ete! An-ne-ete!* (Go out! Go out!)[106]

Hall had little trouble reading from this list: Parry, Lyon, Palmer, Crozier, Fisher (Pe-zart), Mogg, and Henderson. The only one that confused him was "Oo-li-ze," which he admitted he "could not make out." He noted his surprise at not finding a name for James Clark Ross, Crozier's fellow midshipman and friend, on the Inuit list. Eight days later he interviewed old Erktua again. She confirmed that "the Innuits generally pronounce the name Crozier Oo-li-zhar" but added that "there was another Kobluna on board of Parry's ship when at Igloolik whose name was nearly the same. His name was Oo-li-ze … Oo-li-ze was on Parry's vessel – not Lyon's – & lived between aft-cabin & forecastle."[107]

Hall had the crew lists of Parry's ships with him, but he could see no resemblance between any of the men's names and "Oolizhe." He therefore sat down with Erktua and asked her to repeat the names after him. When he reached Crozier, she "pronounced it Oo-li-zhart but on a second attempt she spoke it Cro-zharn." In his usual meticulous fashion, Hall continued down the list and "as Erk-tu-a spoke the name Al-li-son after me or rather *attempted to speak it*, the mystery was instantly unveiled – '*Oo-li-ze*' followed my or rather Parry's Al-li-son!"[108]

Although "Oolizhar" and "Oolizhe" appear similar when written, Hall easily made out the difference, for the names were accented differently. The accent on Crozier's name "Oo-li-zhar" was placed on the first syllable, whereas with "Oolizhe" the accent was placed on the second syllable.[109] Despite the fact that to the Inuit there was little difference between the names "Crozier" and "Allison," Hall attributed all the Oolizhar stories to Crozier, for Allison had not sailed with Franklin. Hall repeatedly stated that during Crozier's earlier voyage as a midshipman, the young sailor had "told the Innuits at Igloolik that he purposed to come into the Innuits country sometime as *Esh-e-mut-ta* (Captain) with a ship or ships & he wished them to tell all Innuits they should meet, that his name was *Ag-loo-ka* & of what he expected to do."[110] This seems out of character, for Crozier was not usually given to bombast or excessive ambition. (For instance, when Franklin was chosen to command the final expedition over him, he wrote, "I sincerely feel I am not equal to the leadership.")[111] It is much more likely that Allison, a "Greenland Master," or pilot, and a captain in his own right, would tell the Inuit that he would soon return with his own ship.

However, John Allison could not have been Tooshooarthariu's "Oolizhe," for he did not sail aboard the *Erebus* or *Terror*. But there was a curious though incorrect tradition among the Pelly Bay Inuit that three of Franklin's men "had formerly been to Ig-loo-lik with Parry."[112] Moreover, the Inuit said that one of Franklin's men had told them that "a great many years before [he] had visited *Iw-wil-lik* (Repulse Bay), *Nu-e-nung-eu-su-a* (Winter Island) & *Ig-loo-lik* with two ships – that while at the latter two places he … got acquainted with a great many of the Innuits."[113]

As far as we know, only Crozier served on both the Parry and Franklin expeditions. And since the Inuit said that they learned the above when some of them visited the *Erebus* and *Terror* before the ships were abandoned, it is probable that Crozier himself told them it. When some of the natives learned how the white men had suffered, they "felt very bad for they had heard how very kind [Crozier] had been to Innuits at Nu-e-nung-eu-ju-a (Winter Island) & Igloolik when he was at those places."[114] Yet it is highly improbable that Crozier was one of the last three survivors, for some of the Inuit traditions from King William Island strongly indicate that he was an early casualty.[115]

Even more intriguing is the fact that by 1869 Hall had begun to doubt whether he had correctly identified "Oolizharn." He felt that he had "surely determined" that the white man who had exchanged names with Aglooka at Igloolik was not Crozier but was James Clark Ross. He noted that "on hearing Ook-pik & Innook-poo-zhe-jook of Neitch-il-le consulting together wherein they frequently pronounced the Kod-lu-nar or European name of Ag-loo-ka ... They both pronounced the name Ross-in though 1st it sounded more like Oo-li-zin, but on my giving a careful ear it was distinctly Ross-in."[116] However, like Allison, James Clark Ross was not a member of Franklin's crew (though, curiously, the Inuit believed that his uncle Sir John was).[117]

So who was Oo-li-zhar/Oo-li-zhen? If such dissimilar names as Crozier, Allison, and Ross sounded similar to the Inuit, it would be foolish to try to place too much reliance on any hypothetical Franklin survivor based on his "kobluna name" alone. There was no shortage of similar-sounding names in the crew lists of the *Erebus* and *Terror*. Almost anyone whose name ended in "son" or "sen" could be a candidate, including Petty Officers John Sullivan (the *Erebus's* captain of the maintop), Alexander Wilson (the *Terror's* carpenter's mate), and John Wilson (captain's coxwain of the *Terror*). On strictly linguistic grounds, perhaps an able seaman from the *Erebus* named William Clossan ("Closs-in"?) should be favoured.

POINTING FINGERS

Perhaps the greatest objection to accepting the eastern Inuit traditions as remembrances of Franklin survivors is the lack of any physical evidence. By disregarding the admittedly uncertain evidence of the "white men's" camps at Parry Bay and Amitoke, critics can point out that there was no tangible corroboration for the Inuit tales. Inuit descriptions of strangers' footprints, clothing, equipment, and mannerisms might be persuasive, but they were inconclusive. Ideally, one would like to find a connected chain of white men's artifacts stretching from King William Island to Repulse Bay. And this is just what we do find.

After entering the ice in 1845, the Franklin expedition had spent a very successful season searching Lancaster Sound and Wellington Channel. Presumably prevented by ice from pursuing his main purpose of discovering a channel leading south towards the known reaches of the continental Arctic coastline, Franklin had taken the *Erebus* and *Terror* to a snug winter anchorage in a sheltered bay behind Beechey Island. In 1850, with the Arctic swarming with searching expeditions, this abandoned wintering station was discovered. A few empty cairns, signs of storehouses ashore, and three graves

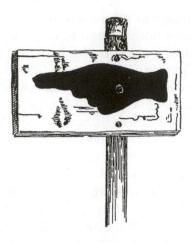

Beechey Island finger post (*Illustrated London News*)

were found. But nothing indicated the direction taken by the missing explorers.

One curious feature of the station at Beechey Island was the presence of "direction posts" made from converted boarding pikes: "No. 1 was bare; No. 2 had an empty potato tin nailed over the top; but No. 3 was very different, for on it was nailed a wooden board thirteen inches wide, upon which in turn was nailed a panel on which had been painted the device of a hand with finger outstretched. This boarding pike was found lying in the snow, minus part of its spike, which was still sticking in the ground, evidently having been fractured by the force of a gale."[118] A similar relic was found at Franklin's Beechey encampment by T.C. Pullen, master of the *North Star*, on 18 August 1853. He described it as "a boarding-pike, painted half white, half black vertically; at one end a piece of board was secured, on which was a hand painted black with forefinger extended."[119] Some searchers believed that the signposts had originally been intended to direct them to the location of Franklin's buried records. Others, noting that Parry had also employed "finger-posts" at Winter Island and Igloolik,[120] concluded that they were simply intended to assist detached parties in locating the ships in a snowstorm.[121]

In 1859 Lieutenant Hobson of McClintock's party was the first to discover the site of a Franklin expedition summer camp near Cape Felix, the northern point of King William Island. He found a large cairn nearby, which had been torn down by the Inuit but still contained a folded but sun-bleached piece of paper.[122] In 1879 Schwatka found another cairn nearby: "The top had been taken down, but in the first course of stones, covered and protected by those thrown from the top, he found a piece of paper with a carefully drawn hand upon it, the index finger at the time pointing in a southerly direction. The bottom part of the paper, on which rested the stone which held it in place, had completely rotted off, so if there had ever been any writing on it that too had disappeared."[123]

A native hunter named Seepunger (or Supunger) told Hall that he had seen a similar cairn near a place called "Shartoo – the flat one." It was "a very high and singular E-nook-shoo-yer (monument), built by kob-lu-nas, of stones, and having at its top a piece of wood something like a hand pointing in a certain direction."[124] This cairn, with its pointing wooden finger, was not found on King William Island. Hall remarked that it was located "not far from Pelly Bay." This questionable identification may have been based on the name Shartoo, for Hall knew that the Simpson Peninsula, which separates Pelly and Committee bays, was also known as "the flat one."[125]

Hall concluded that this evidence of a white man's cairn to the east of King William Island, with the distinctive Franklin pointing finger, was strongly suggestive that some survivors had indeed attempted an overland trek towards Repulse Bay and the Melville Peninsula. Many years later, while travelling with Innookpoozhejook, Hall learned of another curious cairn with a "pointing stone," which the natives had found at Castor and Pollux River.[126] From Seepunger's description of his travels, it is likely that the cairn he saw was in fact a few miles to the north, on a low peninsula that also was known as Shartoo.

Hall believed that some of Franklin's men had visited the cairn at Castor and Pollux River after leaving their ships and that the curious "pointing stone" had served a purpose:

After seeing the direction in wh. this nail pointed to the northward & westward I drew a line in the opposite direction, to the southward & eastward to see if it might not if prolonged, come near to Repulse Bay & found such to be the fact, – therefore the pointing stone may have been intended by those who placed it there, to indicate whence they had come & to what place they were bound. But this latter is of my own conjecture founded upon what In-k has told & upon what information has been derived from some of the Repulse Bay & Igloolik natives.[127]

The cairn at Castor and Pollux River was undoubtedly the one originally built there by Simpson and Dease.[128] They made no mention of any "pointing stone," but it was common practice to place a horizontal stone on top of cairns to make them stand out from the background. This was certainly done by these explorers at the cairn they erected at Cape Herschel on King William Island.[129] Whoever put up the pointing stone, it had been displaced by the time Rae visited it in 1854. Rae described the cairn as "clearly not intended for the protection of property of any kind" and noted that its top had fallen down. The Inuit had previously told him about this cairn, even correctly noting the direction in which the stones had fallen.[130] Built of small stones "in the form of a pillar" the cairn "was not that of the natives," Rae was certain. He spent an hour disassembling it, but "no document was found."[131] Rae does not mention having rebuilt the cairn, nor does he mention a pointing stone.

Hall casually asked Innookpoozhejook "if he ever heard anything about Innuits finding In-nook-shook (Cairn) on Shar-too? (Simpson's & Rae's river between Pelly Bay & sea of Ak-koo-lee) & his response is that he has." According to Innookpoozhejook, some Inuit had "found a monument at E-te-u, with a long stone on top of it pointing in a certain direction & said the monument was not made by Innuits."[132] Excited by yet another instance of a pointing stone, Hall repeatedly returned to the subject in further interviews with Innookpoozhejook:

He said it was at Shar-too, at the same time putting his finger on the Chart & moving it along down the East Coast of Simpson's Peninsula until his finger rested on Point Anderson & Cape Barclay wh. are at the entrance N. side of Keith Bay – & then he said "that is E-to-uki," meaning the projections Point Anderson & Cape Barclay. Then he moved his finger carefully along up the coast till he got to Points J. & R. Clouston or Clouston Pts as they are called in Admiralty Chart when he said that was where that monument was & the stone on top was pointing directly toward a small island that is far out to the Eastward & northward of where the monument was.[133]

Innookpoozhejook remembered the entire sequence of events leading to his discovery of the strange "Innookshoo," and was specific about the timing. By referring to his meetings with Rae at Pelly Bay in 1854, he could date the discovery of this strange monument to 1856.[134] Hall commented: "The story of the peculiarity of this monument as well as the finding of it agrees with what old Kok-lee-arng-nu told me in the spring of 1866, soon after meeting the the [sic] Pelly Bay Innuits," but he did not elaborate.[135]

In Hall's view, these accounts formed a logical sequence, a chain of cairns built or modified by the survivors of the Franklin expedition as they marched eastward towards Repulse Bay. The pointing fingers at Beechey Island and Cape Felix were unquestionably relics of Franklin's men, a kind of trademark. Hall believed that the alignment of the pointing stone on the cairn at Castor and Pollux River was confirmed by Seepunger's "Innookshoo" at Shartoo with the pointing wooden hand and by Innookpoozhejook's at E-te-u with the pointing stone. However, Rae, who had visited all the mentioned places, could not let Hall's dubious reconstruction stand unchallenged. He noted that when he had travelled along the coast of the Simpson Peninsula in 1847, he had reached a point he named "Point Sieveright," which his native guides called E-to-uke.[136] The following day, he left an undescribed "deposit" a few miles north of this.[137] In 1880 Rae attempted to explain Innook-poozhejook's strange monument with the pointing stone, giving a "simple and true version of [Hall's] curious story":

The monument with the stone on top pointing in a certain direction is easily accounted for without bringing any of Franklin's crew such a very long way to build it. By I-vit-chuk's advice we were to cross over land here [at Point Sieveright], as he said the doing so would save us many day's journey. A depot of provisions was to be made for our return, but as we were to follow the coast line on our way back and would not necessarily pass by our "cache" a man was sent to the eastward across Keith Bay with orders to build a conspicuous cairn on Cape Barclay as a guide to our food depot, which was on the low flat western shore of the bay, as a precaution in the event of foggy weather or a change in the aspect of the coast, by snow or other cause. On reference to my narrative (pages 130 and 131) it will be seen how necessary this precaution was, because having the compass bearings between "my cache" and the cairn, I was able without difficulty to make "straight tracks" for our provision depot during the thick weather when on our homeward journey.[138]

Despite Innookpoozhejook's clear testimony that the Inuit found the cairn at least two years after his meeting with Dr Rae in 1854, most historians have agreed with Rae that the cairn at E-te-u/Shartoo was that built by him in 1847, seven years before he met Innook-poozhejook for the first time. It should be noted that Rae makes no mention of having placed a pointing hand or other device on this or any other cairn that his men constructed.

Unknown to Rae, Hall had similarly concluded that E-te-u was "Point Sieveright." However, "on talking with Jerry [Eek-choo-ar-choo] & In-k [Innookpoozhejook] they say that the Cape on Rae's chart wh. he calls Sieveright *is not E-tu-u-ke* but Cape Barclay is E-tu-u-ke." This seems even more conclusive, since Rae's deposit was made at Cape Barclay, not at Point Sieveright. Unfortunately, "In-k says the monument of the Kod-lu-nans (whites) is one day's walking journey above E-tu-uke as the Innuits have told him. In-k never saw this monument himself."[139] The fact that the cairn was found "one day's walking journey" north of Cape Barclay would seem to take the force from Rae's assertion that his man had built it. Hall had originally intended to visit the site of the strange cairn to verify its location and character, but he was prevented by a severe abdominal seizure, during which he thought that his "very life was ebbing."[140]

In the traditional reconstruction of the events, the cairns at Cape Felix are said to have been made by Franklin's men, that at Castor and Pollux River is attributed to Simpson in 1839, and that on the eastern shore of the Simpson Peninsula near Cape Barclay is attributed to Rae in 1847. That Seepunger's monument had a carved wooden pointing hand is ignored, for there is seemingly no allowance for it; or else it is said to have been located not at Shartoo but on King William Island, where Seepunger made other finds. This ignores the fact that there are no known places on King William Island with this name, and that Shartoo was the name of two low peninsulas – one separating Inglis and Spence bays on the mainland to the east of King William Island, and the other separating Pelly and Committee bays even farther east.

AGLOOKA'S HOMECOMING

When Hall first heard the story of Aglooka and his few men sheltering among the Inuit in Tooshooarthariu's care, he was very excited. But after his trip to King William Island and his disillusionment, he lost interest in what became of these survivors. We now know that none of Franklin's men emerged from the Arctic alive, and both

Captain Barry's and Captain Adams's informants were certain that none of the white men survived. Yet the Pelly Bay natives believed that the white men they had seen must have reached safety. Hall found that at Repulse Bay "the Innuits never think they [the white survivors] are dead – do not believe they are."[141]

According to the Inuit, the last two survivors were Crozier (Aglooka) and a "pee-ee-tu" (The latter is usually translated as "steward," but it refers in general to a non-seaman). They remembered that the "pee-ee-tu" was called Nar-tar, and Hall remarked that "on getting the Innuits to try to pronounce the word 'doctor,' they invariably said 'nar-tar.' "[142] This is interesting, especially when we note that the personal relics found farthest from the ships included a medal won by Dr Alexander Macdonald (assistant surgeon aboard the *Terror*)[143] and a piece of wood with "Stanley" scratched on it (Stephen Samuel Stanley was surgeon aboard the *Erebus*).[144]

[Ookbarloo said that] her nephew, Too-she-art-tar-ri-u told her about one man who was with Crozier when he (T.) found him that was Crozier's *Pee-ee-loon*! (that is as Too-koo-li-too says Crozier's *steward* or *waiter* or Mate) Her nephew said he was *very smart* would do anything & everything for Crozier – could hunt good & live like the Innuits. It was not this man that died while Crozier & the three men were with her nephew. Too-koo-li-too now remembers that old See-gar mentioned the fact that Eg-loo-ka (Crozier) & his *Pe-ee-loon* were the two that the Kin-na-pa-too Innuits said had arrived safe among them & had gone to the Kob-lu-na country. She (Too-koo-li-too) further says that she believes from the old lady's description of this man Crozier's *Pee-ee-loon* was "Dr *Ar-pik* as the Innuits of her (T's) country (Northumberland Inlet) called him, but whose name with title really was *Dr. Mcdonald* [sic] of Capt. Penny's ship. "*Ar-pik*" is an Innuit word signifying *smart*, *bright*, *quick* & sometimes even *good-looking*. She (T.) says he liked the Innuits much & they liked him. He could hunt good. Dr Macdonald once wrote a book about her (T.) brother Ee-noo-loo-a-pik. This Macdonald became Surgeon of the "Terror").[145]

The Pelly Bay Inuit did not know what had become of the three men (Aglooka, Arkpik, and their guide), noting that "when Ag-loo-ka & two men left the Innuits nothing more was seen or heard of them afterwards."[146] They indicated that the men had tried to go overland southward to Fort Churchill. Presumably, Aglooka and his party had not passed through Repulse Bay, for the Iwillik Inuit "heard of them some time after from a Kin-na-pa-too, who said he and his people heard shots or reports of guns of strangers somewhere near Chesterfield Inlet."[147] The Inuit hunter named Aglooka confirmed that "all the people here heard long, long time ago that [Aglooka] ... & two men with him had got as far down as the 'Kin-na-pa-too' & had probably got from thence home safe. One of the men that went with Crozier was his pe-e-lood (servant). Heard about this here in this country a little while after Dr Rae went home from Iw-wil-lik 1st time – that's not long after 1847."[148]

As discussed earlier, one of the possible escape routes open to the shipwrecked mariners was the Hudson's Bay Company post at Fort Churchill. Chesterfield Inlet ("the land of the Kinnapatoo") would have to be traversed by any party trying to reach Fort Churchill from the north. The Iwillik natives were certain that this was the way Aglooka went home. Seegar said he had been told by the Kinnapatoo that Aglooka and one companion "arrived among their people & that they (Eg-loo-ka & his men) had gone to where the Kob-lu-nas live – farther down the Big Bay." According to this tale, when Aglooka arrived among the southern Inuit "his powder & shot were nearly all gone," but the Kinnapatoo confirmed that Aglooka and his man "had gone on & had arrived to the nearest place where Kob-lu-nas live," presumably Fort Churchill. Seegar's informants did not have personal knowledge of this, for they "did not see them but said that they had their information from others of their people who did."[149]

The fact that the Repulse Bay natives knew only the two ends of the story – the departure of Aglooka and his two men "from Neitch-il-le" (Boothia Peninsula) and his arrival among the Kinnapatoo of Chesterfield Inlet – suggests that he did not approach Repulse Bay itself. This would imply that Aglooka and his men were not the leaders and sole survivors of the "seventeen men" who had left the ships but were more likely to have been stragglers who had been left behind by those who continued on to Koongwa and Melville Peninsula. Unlike the Repulse natives, who had a justified fear of the Caribou Inuit, the Netsilingmiut of Boothia and Pelly Bay had long ago established an inland trade with these southern bands.

The natives were confident that the white men had arrived home safely. They had, after all, nursed them to health and sent them southward with one of their own people as guide. They knew that the koblunas had arrived among their southern neighbours – the Kinnapatoo. Yet these same Kinnapatoo Inuit, who after 1864 often visited the nearby whalers at Marble Island, insisted that none of the white men in their country had survived.

That Aglooka and his two men bypassed Repulse Bay was seemingly confirmed by Hall, who noted the surprising fact that the Kinnapatoo seemed to learn of the fate of the Franklin expedition before their northern neighbours at Iwillik. He concluded that this "shows that there is a way of communication to the west of this [Repulse Bay], between Neitch-il-lee & Chesterfield Inlet"[150] and that "the Kin-na-pa-toos certainly heard of it before Dr Rae's visit to Repulse Bay & Boothia Felix Peninsula 1853&4! These Innuits say they (the Kin-na-pa-toos) heard it over land, far to the west of Repulse Bay."[151] Hall speculated on this point: "How did the Kin-na-pa-toos get this News? If See-gar's information be true, this question is already answered. I am sure something will be gained by using my very best efforts to get other testimony bearing upon the question: whether Eg-loo-ka did or did not arrive among the Kin-na-pa-too Innuits! See-gar positively says they (the Kin-na-pa-toos) told him (S.) that he (Eg-loo-ka) did."[152]

Seegar confirmed that the Iwillik natives had first learned about Aglooka and his companion from their Pelly Bay (Neitchille) relatives and that only later did they hear that he had arrived in the south. Hall commented: "Said old See-gar on my questioning him about the matter: 'The Kin-na-pa-too Innuits of Chesterfield Inlet told me about *Ag-loo-ka* (Crozier) & of the one man with him of his having arrived arrived [*sic*] among them a long time before. This was a considerable time after Too-shoo-art-thar-u had told me (Seegar) that *Ag-loo-ka was a man that would not starve.*'"[153]

Rae again believed that he was the Aglooka referred to by the Kinnapatoo.[154] However, as with all the stories we have investigated, there are obvious points of discrepancy between the Inuit reminiscences and the known activities of the famous explorer. Rae, himself a medical doctor, may have been "nartar"; but if so, who in the party was Aglooka – the leader? An independent man who was disdainful of creature comforts, Rae never went to the Arctic accompanied by a servant or steward. And when he travelled through the Kinnapatoo lands, he was accompanied not by one companion but by many: by ten men in two boats in 1846–47, and by thirteen (of whom seven were sent back from Chesterfield

Inlet) in 1854.[155] Rae apparently never met any natives near Chesterfield Inlet, merely passing by in his boats. He did not hunt with them, although he was a proficient hunter. A steadfastly self-sufficient traveller, Rae was never "in distress," and he certainly never met a party of natives when "his powder and shot were nearly all gone."

We thus return to the same point at which we started when investigating Kia's story – if the stranger seen by the Kinnapatoo Inuit was not Rae, who could the man be? Hall wondered in his journal what had prevented Aglooka, who knew everything the Inuit could teach him about survival in their land, from reaching the settlements on Hudson Bay. The only answer he could think of was that Aglooka and his companion *"were murdered by the Kin-na-pa-toos*, for, according to the accounts of the Innuits with whom I have so far wintered, they (the Kin-na-pa-toos) are a *treacherous* people."[156]

There was circumstantial evidence for Hall's poor opinion of the Kinnapatoo Inuit. He records that his Iwillik informants told him of how the Kinnapatoo tried to enlist them in a plot to attack the two whaling ships commanded by the Chapel brothers in 1860–61. The motive for the proposed massacre was simple greed – to obtain all the treasures of the white men. Hall later informed his friend Captain Chapel of this threat to his safety, and Chapel said he had been aware of the plot at the time.[157]

Shortly before leaving the Arctic, Hall received information from Captain Fisher of the whaler *Ansel Gibbs* which confirmed his suspicions:

I here note what information I have received from Capt. Fisher relative to what he had heard about Crozier's arrival & death in the locality of Chesterfield Inlet, while he (Capt. Fisher) was in Winter Quarters at Marble Island (this last winter 1868–9).

The information, Captain Fisher said, was drawn out of *"Kin-na-pa-toos"* – Innuits that are natives along the locality of Chesterfield Inlet – who from time to time came over the ice from the main land to Marble Island to visit the ships there. The sense & substance as communicated to me is that a white man arrived among the Kin-na-pa-toos many years ago & that he was finally murdered – or what was the same – was starved to death – & *this white man*, Capt. Fisher says, *was Crozier*. Another white man was with Crozier but he died before getting among the Kin-na-pa-toos. How Capt. F. knows that the white man that was murdered was Crozier, he did not tell me ... Capt. F. said that it was quite impossible to get the old Innuits to tell anything about the matter but what information he did get was out of younger ones.[158]

Conclusion

Almost one hundred and thirty years ago an eccentric explorer with little formal education and no experience answered what he believed was a "call from God" to hurry to the North. He believed he would find some survivors of the Franklin expedition still living with the Inuit of the central Arctic. Setting aside the objections that the men had been missing for almost twenty years and that tales of their demise had been heard and largely confirmed five years earlier, Hall pursued his quixotic quest with admirable determination and perseverance.

For four years he lived with the Inuit, sharing their lifestyle and listening to their stories. He carefully recorded their tales of strange white men and could not contain his joy when told that there were "four who did not die." He heard from Ouela about the "kind-hearted and forever to be praised" Tooshooarthariu, who had sheltered the last survivors for a winter and then sent them towards home with a native guide. He learned of meat caches, which had been robbed by unknown strangers, and of monuments with pointing rocks or finger-shaped indicators which had not been built by native hands. He listened carefully to tales of outward-pointing footprints in the ice and snow, and of fearful "Etkerlin" (Indians) who were thought to have been "kobluna" (white men).

In 1868 Hall first heard the story of Kia and concluded that "Kia saw what I have not the least doubt was one of Sir John Franklin's men."[1] After questioning the Iwillik natives closely, he wrote: "The news relative to there having been seen white men near Ig-loo-lik between 1849 and 1865, proves to be true beyond all question in my mind."[2] On his arrival at South Ooglit Island, Hall found one hundred Inuit and began interviewing them, "at first separately and then at a time when quite a party were gathered in his igloo." According to Nourse, "he was further strengthened in his belief of what he had heard about the white men seen on the southern shores of the Strait. He seems to have really expected that he would soon find some of Franklin's men still alive."[3] The information Hall later acquired from Kia's friends Koolooa, Kudloon, Artungun, and others seemed to solidify his belief. He was to write that "one statement may here be made that White men have been living on Melville Peninsula for several years & *no man knowing what I do can possibly believe otherwise.* They are part of the lost companions of Sir John Franklin."[4]

By the time Hall returned from King William Island in 1869, however, he had begun to doubt whether any of Franklin's men had survived. On King William Island he had interviewed Tooshooarthariu's hunting companions and had learned that at least one party of white men had been "heartlessly" abandoned to their fate. Tired and frustrated by his lack of success, he concluded that much of the Inuit testimony was inherently unreliable. Nevertheless, he offered no explanation for the Melville Peninsula stories and could not bring himself to believe that they were recollections of Rae and Parry rather than the Franklin survivors. Later historians, aware that Hall was wary of the truth of the accounts he had collected, tended to discount them. Cyriax voiced the common opinion when he remarked that "the correctness of Hall's final conclusion, that there had never been any survivors of the Franklin expedition, appears to be entirely beyond question."[5]

Hall was quick to jump to conclusions and was not averse to prodigious feats of logical contortion in his efforts to make contradictory evidence amenable to his preconceived ideas. One eminent modern scholar considered the Melville Peninsula stories to be "a good example of the problems Hall ignored when he accepted Eskimo reminiscences at face value ... In spite of Hall's attempts to consider other interpretations, he usually allowed most of what he heard to fall into a preconceived pattern: Crozier and some other survivors from the *Erebus* and *Terror* went east from King William

Island and continued to survive for many years near Fury and Hecla Strait. That was the way he wanted it to be."[6]

Even so, historians may have been too hasty in abandoning Hall's
theory of survivors in the east. Although there are definite points of
similarity between some of the Inuit tales and the activities of known
explorers, there are also disturbing discrepancies; and while the tradition preserved under Tooshooarthariu's name is not unimpeach-
able, the accounts heard by Captains Adams, Barry, and Fisher seem
to corroborate some of what Hall was told.

Quite apart from Hall's conclusions concerning Franklin survivors, the question remains, "Who did the Inuit see?" No one has
ever claimed that the Inuit were liars. The detail and accuracy of
their reports have convinced all investigators that they were describing actual contacts with white men. We have seen that a good
case can be made that the Inuit reminiscences related to expeditions by Parry and Rae. Yet some doubts remain, for details that do
not fit these scenarios confound us, as does the overarching consideration that the Inuit knew about both these explorers in great detail and would not have been likely to confuse them with unknown
strangers.

The physical evidence is difficult to attribute: the campsite and
cairn in Parry Bay are unaccounted for; the cache at E-te-u was possibly Rae's; and the campsite by the lake at Amitoke was possibly
Lyon's. Yet the details continue to nag at us. It is hard to believe that
Tookoolitoo mistook an Inuit tenting place for one made by white
men, that a grown Artungun found the remains of a decades-old
fish dinner, or that the characteristic arnuk found by Armouyer was
not left by white men. And one struggles to explain red-painted
cans and a white man's dog in the highlands of Amitoke.

Despite the problems, the overall chronology of the Inuit tales is
remarkably consistent. The dates of the strange encounters are invariably arrived at by reference to Rae's two expeditions, most of the
reminiscences being bracketed by them. Although the conclusion
that some of Franklin's men could still have been alive as late as 1852
seems unlikely, since this was four years after the *Erebus* and *Terror*
were abandoned near Victory Point, other Inuit testimony indicates
that the sighting of strange white men may have occurred as little as
one year after the arrival of the (manned?) Franklin ship at "Shartoo."[7] These dates seem to discount Parry and Lyon as sources and
to point to Rae. The problem is that Parry was in the right place for

Artungun's reminiscences but was thirty years too soon; Rae's timing was (almost) right, but with the exception of Kia's tale and the Iwillik/Christie stories, there is no evidence that he ever approached the right areas.

Historians have almost universally accepted that Rae or Parry must have been the inspiration for the stories of white men that Hall heard. None has seen any reason to support Hall's contention that the stories must have refered to Franklin's men. The "standard reconstruction" of the fate of the Franklin expedition asserts that all Crozier's men died in the summer and fall of 1848, either on King William Island or on the adjoining mainland, and that none of them ever proceeded east of the Great Fish River.

I have elsewhere argued that this is too simplistic and that it is not supported by the Inuit testimony about the white men on King William Island (Kikertuk). Any reconstruction that takes all the Inuit traditions into account is led ineluctably to the conclusion that the 1848 abandonment was only the first in a series, that the Inuit first encountered the ships in 1849, and that the last ship sank (at a place the Inuit called Ootjoolik, somewhere in the vicinity of Kirkwall Island) shortly after the last few survivors left, probably in 1851.[8]

Dealing with the evidence collected by Hall on the Melville Peninsula is difficult. Not all of it survives. Nourse laconically remarked that "the details of his conversations were written out with great care in a full journal" but that in 1871 this "was irrecoverably lost in some unaccountable way."[9] Only Hall's sled notes and some incomplete extracts of this journal (copied for the benefit of Lady Franklin and since known as books A and B) are available for researchers. In consequence, some traditions that Hall mentions are known only from oblique references, the full particulars having been recorded elsewhere.

In 1879 the various documents of the Hall Collection were edited and prepared for publication by Professor J.E. Nourse. This edited edition has been the basis for most modern commentary, but it is only when Hall's evidence is taken in its entirety that some of his more questionable conclusions seem less far-fetched. Nourse's work, although well done, was incomplete; yet most historians have used it in arriving at their conclusions, since the Hall Collection itself is large and unindexed. While Nourse was exceptionally precise in transcribing Hall's work, confining himself to the addition of punctuation and the correction of the most egregious errors of spelling or usage, nevertheless there is much of value that he did not deem "worthy" of inclusion in his long book. Since Nourse's work is widely available and is familiar to scholars and general readers, I have quoted it extensively, always checking the original documents in the Hall Collection and inserting corrections or clarifications where necessary.

Hall's evidence from King William Island can be compared with that collected by his predecessors (Rae and McClintock) and his successors (Frederick Schwatka and Knud Rasmussen among others). As the undoubted focus of the tragedy, King William Island was carefully searched by them and the natives assiduously and repeatedly interviewed. Such cross-comparisons are fruitful, and although discrepancies sometimes appear, in general the traditions collected by the various explorers were complementary and consistent, even if their conclusions were not.

Melville Peninsula, on the other hand, is far from the supposed site of the disaster, and Hall's brief three-month journey there stands alone. We must therefore always bear in mind that we have no sources of corroboration or verification for the traditional tales he collected. This does not completely invalidate the Melville Peninsula stories, for if Hall's King William Island work is any yardstick, he seems to have been a particularly careful and accurate recorder of Inuit testimony, largely because of the excellence of his interpreters.

If the stories of the Etkerlin were not about Rae or Parry, there seem to be only three alternatives. The first is that the Etkerlin were, as their name implies, Indians. This was almost always the Inuit explanation, at least initially, though they often admitted that the actions and artifacts had more of a "kobluna" character. Some of the stories would fit this scenario, but others would not (the fact that Kia's stranger had a white face, and that Indians did not eat from red-painted tin canisters).

A second explanation for the strange white men who seem to have wandered on the Melville Peninsula would be that they were lost whalers. "Officially," the whalers did not reach the Gulf of Boothia or the upper reaches of Hudson Bay until the 1860s, but in view of the poorly documented and secretive nature characteristic of this trade, it is not inconceivable that a pioneering vessel could have come to grief in the area during the preceding decade. If this occurred, however, there is no knowledge of it; the exhaustive investigation I made failed to identify any suitable lost or missing whalers in the appropriate timeframe.

The third possibility is that Hall, admittedly for many of the wrong reasons, was correct in his preconceived notion of Franklin survivors. The trail of the "great Captain" and his few companions is tenuous, as we would expect it to be. But although it is unprovable, the idea that a few men (and their dog) attempted an impossible escape from a terrible disaster is compelling. In this scenario, the survivors of the disaster at King William Island arrive at Pelly Bay in their effort to reach Iwillik/Repulse Bay. Presumably, their aim is to get to either Pond Bay or Churchill. Aglooka and two or three men fall behind and are found and cared for by "Tooshooarthariu" for one winter. The next year, they are sent southward to the perhaps-murderous Kinnapatoo. The other white men continue along, build a cairn at E-te-u, rob and terrify the natives near Rae Isthmus, and later divide into two contingents. One of these, perhaps ignorant of the geography, continues to follow the shore and proceeds up the west coast of the Melville Peninsula (to be seen by Kia and Koolooa). The other group crosses the Rae Isthmus, leaving footprints at Iwillik, *arnuk* on the highlands, and a campsite at Amitoke. These men are eventually seen (and avoided) near Igloolik (at Nelikiokbig) and Ingnearing.

These northbound survivors were possibly aware from Parry's accounts that the Igloolik Inuit were only four days' journey from friends at Admiralty Inlet, who in turn were in contact with the whalers at Pond Bay. These men, searching for the route up Gifford Fiord, may have wandered too far south and ended up in the vicinity of Murray Maxwell Bay and Steensby Inlet ("Ingnearing"), where they eventually died. According to Armou, the Etkerlin who tried to go farther north also succumbed to starvation and exposure.

The strangers were seen repeatedly. At Koongwa they searched for a way across the lake. At Ingnearing they were seen as terrifying shapes against the horizon. Farther north they laughed and waved at the frightened boys at Amitoke and were also seen striding purposefully towards Cape Englefield. These men who, years after most of their comrades had died, had learned enough of the lessons of survival to bring them hundreds of miles, very nearly managed to escape to safety.

Whether this is held to be truth or fantasy will depend on each individual's evaluation of the conflicting and difficult evidence. The explorers and their Inuit friends have passed from the scene, as have the mysteries of unknown and challenging shores and the wonder of folk-tales told during the long Arctic night. The stories of the Etkerlin will probably never be completely explained. Nevertheless, as the Inuit knew, the best stories are those that survive on their own merit, and bear endless repetition.

APPENDIX

Inuit Terms and Place Names

Variations are given in parentheses

Adge-go (Adg-go)   Fury and Hecla Strait

Aglooka (Aglooga, Eglooka, Aklukaq)   "the one who takes long strides"; name commonly given to white explorers, including Parry, James Clark Ross, Rae, and possibly Francis Crozier

Agwiperwik (Agwisseowik). See *Og-big-seer-ping*

Akkoolee (Akule, Accoolee)   "the delta bay, the bay into which many rivers empty"; Committee Bay

Amitoke (Amitioke, Amitsoq, Amitsuq, Ar-ni-toke)   "the narrow one"; peninsula on the east coast of Melville Peninsula, approximately halfway between Igloolik and Repulse Bay

Angeko (angatkut, anatkoq, angekok, attangut)   shaman. The act of summoning the spirits was "ankooting"

Ar-lang-nuk (Alarniq)   southeastern point of Hooper Inlet, west of Igloolik. Parry had a camp here and set up his famous "flagpost" nearby

Ark-pik   "smart" or "quick"; Inuit name for Dr Alexander Macdonald of HMS *Terror*

Arlangnazhu (Arlangnazhoo)   Garry Bay

Arnuk (ar-nuk)   dung

Arviligjuaq (Arviligjop tarajua)   "the big one with whales"; Pelly Bay

E-ju-eek-too   place on north shore of Repulse Bay to the east of Iwillik

E-te-u (E-tu-uke, E-to-uki, E-tee-u-oki)   Cape Barclay

Eshemuta (Isumataq, Ishumatar) "he who thinks for others"; leader, usually translated as "chief" for the Inuit, or "Captain" in relation to white men

Eshemutanar "little Eshemuta"; used for a subordinate officer

Est-shu-tin arctic moss (Andromeda Tetragona), used as fuel

Etkerlin (Itqilît, Itqidlit, Ik-kil-lin) Indians

Igloolik (Iglulik, Igluligarjuk) "the place where there are many igloos" – island off the east coast of Melville Peninsula; modern village and traditional habitation of Inuit, first visited by Parry and Lyon, who wintered their ships there during the winter of 1822–23

Ikkee-rei-seuk (Agssarneq) Chesterfield Inlet

Ilivileq Adelaide Peninsula

Ingnearing (Ingnerit, Ingnertoq, Ingnertuq) a location north of Amitoke on the east coast of Melville Peninsula; also a place on the northern shore of Steensby Inlet (Baffin Island)

Innookshoo (Enookshooyer, Inukshuk, Inuksut) cairn or monument, a common type being a pillar with "arms" intended to represent a human and to frighten caribou into ambush

Iwillik (Aivilik, Ayweelik, Eiwillik) traditional Inuit campsite in Repulse Bay; used as a general determinative for that bay (see *Naujan*)

Kangek-loo Quilliam Creek

Kee-gee-wee inland location to the west of Amitoke

Kikertak (Kikituk, Kikertung, Ki-ki-tung, Qeqertarjuaq) "the big island"; King William Island

Kingmetokebig (Qimmiqtugvik, Kingmetovik) locality on the east coast of Melville Peninsula, four miles north of the modern village of Hall Beach

Kinnapatoo (Kenepetu) thought to mean "it is wet," a nickname for the Qairnirmiut (Qaernermiut) Inuit of the Wager Bay region

Kobluna (kodluna, kabloona, qavdlunar) white man

Kok "the river"; Castor and Pollux River

Kommotik sled

Konajuk "the big river"; Back or Great Fish River

Kongma (Kung-moo) dwelling with snow walls and canvas or skin top

Konuaq "the little river"; Hayes River

Kooloota (kuluta) coat

Koongwa (Koong-wa, Koon-wa) narrows joining Christie and North Pole lakes (Rae Isthmus)

Melokeeta (Melokuta, Mallookhitta, Malluke-se-ta) Lyon Inlet

Nanook (nanuk) white (polar) bear

Naujan (Nowyarn) traditional Inuit campsite on the northern shore of Repulse Bay a few miles to the east of Aivilik; site of Hall's campsite and now used as the modern Inuit name of Repulse Bay (see *Iwillik*)

Ne-yu-ning Eit-du-a (Nu-e-nung-eu-su-a)   Winter Island

Neitchille (Nacilik, Netsilik)   "the one with seals"; Willerstedt Lake in the Boothian Isthmus. The name was used by explorers and Inuit for the entire Boothian Peninsula. The Netsilingmiut, or "seal people," took their name from this lake in the centre of their hunting grounds

Nelikiokbig   highlands to the east of Igloolik and south of Quilliam Creek

Netchuk (nacheq)   seal

Nowyer (nauja)   white gull

Nuvuk (Noowook)   Inuit encampment on the coast of Hudson Bay south of Wager Bay

Og-big-seer-ping   place on Melville Peninsula to the northwest of the South Ooglit Islands, described as "highlands"

Ok-kee-bee-jee-loo-a   name used by Hall for Pelly Bay, probably denotes a locality there (see *Arviligjuaq*)

Ooglit (Uglit)   two sets of islands near the east coast of Melville Peninsula. The South Ooglit Islands lie approximately four miles north of Amitoke, and the North Ooglit Islands are approximately thirty miles farther north

Ook-soo-see-too   shore on the west coast of Adelaide Peninsula, near where the second Franklin ship sank

Ook-soo-yer (Oqssorioq)   Marble Island

Ootgoolik (Ujulik)   "the one abounding in bearded seals"; Queen Maud Gulf

Ootkooseek   women's stone pot. Discarded tin canisters left by the explorers were often used as pots and shared the same name

Ootkooseekalik (Ootkooseek-salik, Oot-ke-ish-e-lik, Oot-koo-ish-e-lik, Ook-koo-i-hi-ca-lik, Utkuhigjalik)   the estuary of the Back River (Chantrey Inlet); also the name of Wager Bay

Ou-ye-too   freshwater ice

Pee-ee-tu (pee-ee-loon)   non-seaman, interpreted by Hall as servant or steward

Ping-it-ka-lik   locality on the east coast of Melville Peninsula, between Amitoke and Igloolik

Pitikzhee   bow

Pitiulak   Depot Island

Qatiktalik   Cape Fullerton

See-er-wa-ark-chu   a locality two miles west of the entrance to the narrows leading into Murray Maxwell Bay (Baffin Island)

Appendix

See-nee locality near Cape Berens on west coast of Pelly Bay, home of the fierce Seeneemiute Inuit

Seejokbig north end of Miles Lake (Rae Isthmus)

Shartoo (Shatook, Satoq) "the flat one"; name given to many localities, including a place on the west coast of the Adelaide Peninsula, the peninsula dividing Spence Bay and Inglis Bay, Simpson Peninsula, and Prince of Wales (now called Wales) Island

Shaylavou lie

Tes-su-e-ark (Teisuksowak) large lake near east coast of Melville Peninsula (now Hall Lake)

Timanat (timanato, tineenatu) "the same as"

Toodnoo fat

Tooktoo (tukto) caribou (reindeer)

Toonoonee (tununeq) "the back of beyond"; Pond Inlet

Toonooneeroochuk Admiralty Inlet

Tupik (tupeq) tent

Notes

CHAPTER ONE

1 Sir John Ross, *Narrative of a Second Voyage in Search of a Northwest Passage*; T. Simpson, *Narrative of Discoveries on the North Coast of North America*; Woodman, *Unravelling the Franklin Mystery*, 11–23.

2 National Maritime Museum, Arctic Collection, doc. 2/121.

3 Cyriax, "The Two Franklin Expedition Records Found on King William Island," 179; Hall Collection, 58919, 14 July 1866.

4 National Maritime Museum, Arctic Collection, doc. 2/121.

5 Stackpole, *The Long Arctic Search*, 75–6; Cyriax, "Recently Discovered Traces of Sir John Franklin's Expedition," 212.

6 Rae to Barclay, 1 September 1854, in Rae, *Doctor John Rae's Correspondence*, 274–6.

7 McClintock, *Voyage of the "Fox."*

8 Loomis, *Weird and Tragic Shores*, 27.

9 Ibid., 35–7.

10 Ibid., 39.

11 Ibid., 41.

12 Ibid.

13 Ibid., 44.

14 Woodman, *Unravelling the Franklin Mystery*, 319–24.

15 Museum of Armed Forces History, Smithsonian Institution, Washington, Hall Collection (hereafter, Hall Collection), 58937, booklet no. 38, 18 May 1869; Woodman, *Unravelling the Franklin Mystery*, 123–38.

16 Woodman, *Unravelling the Franklin Mystery*, 6–7.

17 Hall Collection, 58919, 4 May 1866.

18 Hall Collection, 58937, booklet no. 28, 9 May 1869; Nourse, *Narrative of the Second Arctic Expedition*, 404; McClintock, *Voyage of the "Fox,"* 227.

19 Hall Collection, 58937, booklet no. 22, 2 May 1869.

20 Ibid., booklet no. 28, 8 May 1869.

21 Fluhmann, *Second in Command*, 101.

22 The name "Ki-a" (as recorded by Hall) is derived from the word for an Inuit hunter's boat, which is commonly rendered into English as "kayak."

23 Hall Collection, 58936, 7 April 1868.

24 Ibid., 9 April 1868.

25 Ibid., 17 February 1868.

26 Ibid., 8 May 1868.

27 Ibid., 24 April 1868.

28 Nourse, *Narrative of the Second Arctic Expedition*, 332.

29 In August 1822 Parry dispatched various parties to search Fury and Hecla Strait. Lieutenants Reid and Bushnan and Midshipman Crozier were all sent to the area indicated, Crozier to conduct tidal observations. In addition, a "temporary light house" was erected on the east point of Amherst Island. Either the remaining base of this or a temporary shelter built by the others could explain these strange structures. See Parry, *Journal of a Second Voyage*, 350.

30 Nourse, *Narrative of the Second Arctic Expedition*, 332–3.

31 Hall Collection, 58936, 19 February 1868.

32 Ibid.

33 Ibid., 17 February 1868.

34 Ibid., 8 May 1868.

35 Ibid., 7 April 1868.

36 Hall Collection, 58913, book A, 61–2. The hunters were named Kia, Koolooa, Kud-loon, O-kay, Suk-bar-bing, Muk-ta, Kop-poo, and Soo-blu-ar-u.

37 Ibid., 36–7; 58933, booklet no. 28, 1–2, 98–100.

38 Hall Collection 58913, book A, 34.

39 Ibid., 54.

40 Ibid., 34–5.

41 Ibid., 36–9.

42 Ibid., 50.

43 Nourse, *Narrative of the Second Arctic Expedition*, 332.

44 Hall Collection, 58913, book B, 115.

45 Ibid., book A, 54.

46 Ibid., book B, 115.

47 Ibid., book A, 64–6.

48 Ibid., book B, 115.

49 Ibid., book A, 64–6.

50 Ibid., 51–2.

51 Hall Collection, 58936, 7 April 1868.

52 Hall Collection, 58913, book A, 63.

53 Hall Collection, 58936, 25 April 1868.

54 Hall Collection, 58913, book B, 115–17.

55 Ibid., book A, 63–4.

56 Ibid., 117.

57 Hall Collection, 58933, booklet no. 28, 13 May 1868, 43–8; 58913, book A, 50.

58 Hall Collection, 58933, booklet no. 28, 9 April 1868, 1–2; 58913, book A, 36.

59 Hall Collection, 58933, booklet no. 28, 15 May 1868, 49–55; 58913, book A, 60.

60 Hall Collection, 58933, booklet no. 28, 11 January 1868, 98–100; 58913, book B, 113–17.

61 Ibid., book A, 52.

62 Ibid., 53.

63 Ibid., 39.

64 Ibid., 39–40.

65 Rae, *Doctor John Rae's Correspondence*, xxxi.

66 Hall Collection, 58913, book A, 57–8.

67 Ibid., 56–7.

68 Bunyan et al., *No Ordinary Journey*, 82.

69 Cyriax, "Captain Hall and the So-called Survivors," 170.

70 Ibid., 175.

71 Scott Polar Research Institute, MS 787/1, Rae, unpublished autobiography.

72 *Orkney Herald*, 16 February 1887; Rae, *Doctor John Rae's Correspondence*, xiv.

73 Wallace, "Rae of the Arctic," 28.

74 Ballantyne, *Hudson's Bay*, 225–6; Rae, *Doctor John Rae's Correspondence*, xix.

75 Rae, *Doctor John Rae's Correspondence*, xxix–xxx.

76 Ibid., 41.

77 Rae, *Narrative of an Expedition*, 6, 137–8, and *Doctor John Rae's Correspondence*, 47.

78 Rae to *New York Herald*, dated 23 May and published 4 July 1880.

79 Rae, *Doctor John Rae's Correspondence*, 41.

80 Ibid.

81 Hall Collection, 58915, 22 November 1865, 317; Rae, *Narrative of an Expedition*, 75.

82 Rae, *Narrative of an Expedition*, 149.

83 Cyriax, "Captain Hall and the So-called Survivors," 175.

84 Rae, *Doctor John Rae's Correspondence*, 63.

85 Rae, *Narrative of an Expedition*, 155.

86 Ibid., 155–6.

87 Ibid., 156.

88 Rae, *Doctor John Rae's Correspondence*, 65.

89 Ibid.

90 Nourse, *Narrative of the Second Arctic Expedition*, 431.

91 Cyriax, "Captain Hall and the So-called Survivors," 184.

92 Loomis, *Weird and Tragic Shores*, 34.

93 Wallace, "Rae of the Arctic," 33.

94 Rae, *Doctor John Rae's Correspondence*, cvi.

95 Wallace, "Rae of the Arctic," 33.

96 Ibid., 29.

97 Rae, *Doctor John Rae's Correspondence*, ciii.

98 Stefansson, "Rae's Arctic Correspondence," 36.

99 Ibid., 37.

100 Wallace, "Rae of the Arctic," 33.

101 Rae to *New York Herald*, dated 23 May and published 4 July 1880.

102 Ibid.

103 Ibid.

104 Hall Collection, 58937, booklet no. 6, 5 April 1869.

105 Ibid., booklet no. 19, 28 April 1869.

106 Rae, "Letter of Dr. John Rae to the British Admiralty," 284.

107 Rae to *New York Herald*, dated 23 May and published 4 July 1880.

108 Ibid.

109 Neatby, "Joe and Hannah," 17.

110 Ibid.; Loomis, *Weird and Tragic Shores*, 86–7.

111 Cyriax, "Captain Hall and the So-called Survivors," 170.

112 Rae to *New York Herald*, dated 23 May and published 4 July 1880.

113 Ibid.

114 Rae, "Letter of Dr. John Rae to the British Admiralty," 285.

115 Hall Collection, 58936, 17 April 1868; Nourse, *Narrative of the Second Arctic Expedition*, 333.

116 Rae to *New York Herald*, dated 23 May and published 4 July 1880.

117 Hall Collection, 58914, 8 December 1864, 219–20.

118 Parry, *Journal of a Second Voyage*, 208.

119 Ibid., 513.

120 Hall Collection, 58913, book A, 36–7.

121 Ibid., book B, 115.

122 Ibid., 114.

123 Ibid., book A, 35.

124 Hall Collection, 58936, booklet no. 31, 3–7 April 1868; 58913, book A, 52.

125 Hall Collection 58936, booklet no. 31, 21–2 April 1868.

126 Ibid., 24 April 1868.

127 Ibid., 21–2 April 1868.

128 Ibid., 20 April 1868.

129 Nourse, *Narrative of the Second Arctic Expedition*, 547.

130 Hall Collection, 58936, 24 April 1868.

131 Ibid., 5 May 1868; 58933, 74.

132 Hall Collection, 58936, 8 April 1868.

133 Hall Collection, 58913, book A, 54.

134 Ibid., 34–5.

135 Rae, *Narrative of an Expedition*, 155.

136 Rae, *Doctor John Rae's Correspondence*, 65.

137 Ibid., 62.

138 Hall Collection, 58913, book A, 39.

139 Hall Collection, 58913, book A, 1–3.

140 Nourse, *Narrative of the Second Arctic Expedition*, 342, 547.

141 Ibid., 346; Hall Collection, 58936, booklet no. 31, 24 April 1868.

142 Nourse, *Narrative of the Second Arctic Expedition*, 344.

143 Hall Collection, 58936, 25 April 1868.

144 Nourse, *Narrative of the Second Arctic Expedition*, 346–7; Hall Collection, 58936, booklet no. 31, 25 April 1868.

145 Nourse, *Narrative of the Second Arctic Expedition*, 345.

146 Ibid., 347–8.

147 Hall Collection, 58936, 25 April 1868.

148 Rae, *Narrative of an Expedition*, 155–6.

149 Rae, "Letter of Dr. John Rae to the British Admiralty," 284–5.

150 Ibid., 288.

151 Ibid., 287.

152 Cyriax, "Captain Hall and the So-called Survivors of the Franklin Expedition," 175.

153 Ibid., 176–7.

154 Parry, *Journal of a Second Voyage*, 17, 51, 271.
155 Cyriax, "Captain Hall and the So-called Survivors of the Franklin Expedition," 177.
156 Hall Collection, 58936, 25 April 1868.
157 Rae to *New York Herald*, dated 23 May and published 4 July 1880.
158 Cyriax, "Captain Hall and the So-called Survivors of the Franklin Expedition," 177.

CHAPTER TWO

1 Hall Collection, 58936, 17 April 1868.
2 Ibid., 19 February 1868.
3 Parry, *Journal of a Second Voyage*, 89–92.
4 Hall Collection, 58936, 19 February 1868.
5 Hall Collection, 58937, booklet no. 53, 11 June 1869.
6 Birket-Smith, *The Caribou Eskimos*, 165.
7 Rasmussen, *The Netsilik Eskimos*, 121–7.
8 Parry, *Journal of a Second Voyage*, 391; Lyon, *Lyon's Private Journal*, 153.
9 Hall Collection, 58936, 8 April 1868.
10 Hall Collection, 58913, book A, 42–4; Nourse, *Narrative of the Second Arctic Expedition*, 605.
11 Hall Collection, 58913, book A, 45.
12 Hall Collection, 58936, 19 February 1868.
13 Ibid.
14 Hall Collection, 58937, 23 March 1869.
15 Gilder, *Schwatka's Search*, 310.
16 American Museum of Natural History, Comer Papers, George Comer's, Journal, no. 8, 10. I am indebted to Mr Edmund Carpenter of the Rock Foundation, New York, for bringing this tale to my attention.
17 Hall Collection, 58936, 19 February 1868.
18 Hall Collection, 58913, book A, 44.
19 Hall Collection, 58936, 19 February 1868.
20 Hall Collection, 58936, 7 April 1868.
21 Rae, *Narrative of an Expedition*, 60.
22 Ibid., 49–50.
23 Rae to *New York Herald* dated 23 May and published 4 June 1880.
24 Rae, *Narrative of an Expedition*, 68.
25 Ibid., 99–100.

26 Rae to *New York Herald* dated 23 May and published 4 June 1880.

27 Hall Collection, 58915, 23 February 1866; Rae, *Doctor John Rae's Correspondence*, lxxix–lxxx.

28 Rae, "The Lost Arctic Voyagers," 434.

29 Stefansson, "Rae's Arctic Correspondence," 37.

30 Rae to *New York Herald* dated 23 May and published 4 June 1880.

31 Rae, "Sir John Franklin and His Crews," 19–20.

32 Rae, "Rae on the Eskimos," 40.

33 Hall Collection, 58937, booklet no. 3, 27 March 1869.

34 Ibid., booklet no. 4, 31 March 1869.

35 Hall Collection, 58913, book A, 45.

36 Ibid., 48.

37 Hall Collection, 58915, 330.

38 Ibid., 34.

39 Hall Collection, 58913, book B, 76–7.

40 Ibid., 78.

41 Ibid., 80–2.

42 Hall's "E-ju-eed-too" may be Rasmussen's small peninsula called "Ibjugiktoq," and "Oog-la-ri-zaur Island" is best identified by the nearby island "uklertjuk" (Rasmussen, *Iglulik and Caribou Eskimo Texts*, 94).

43 Hall Collection, 58913, book B, 82–5.

44 Hall Collection, 58937, booklet no. 45, 29 May 1869.

45 Ibid.

46 Rae, "Rae on the Eskimos," 40.

47 Hall Collection, 58913, book A, 5; Parry, *Journal of a Second Voyage*, 161, 173–4.

48 Nourse, *Narrative of the Second Arctic Expedition*, 301.

49 Parry, *Journal of a Second Voyage*, 398.

50 Ibid., 204.

51 Hall Collection, 58913, book A, 6–9; Nourse, *Narrative of the Second Arctic Expedition*, 597–8.

52 Mathiassen, *Material Culture of the Iglulik Eskimos*, 31. The southern point of Grant-Suttie Bay is now named Ignerit Point.

53 Hall Collection, 58915, 74.

54 Rasmussen, *Intellectual Culture of the Iglulik Eskimos*, endpaper map; Mathiassen, *Material Culture of the Iglulik Eskimos*, 29–30.

55 Hall Collection, 58913, book A, l7–19; Nourse, *Narrative of the Second Arctic Expedition*, 598.

56 Hall Collection, 58913, book B, 87–90.

57 Ibid., 90.

58 Ibid., book A, 9–11; Nourse, *Narrative of the Second Arctic Expedition*, 598–9.

59 Hall Collection, 58913, book A, 18; Nourse, *Narrative of the Second Arctic Expedition*, 602.

60 Hall Collection, 58913, book A, 33–4; Nourse, *Narrative of the Second Arctic Expedition*, 603.

61 Hall Collection, 58913, book A, 12–14; Nourse, *Narrative of the Second Arctic Expedition*, 599; Parry, *Journal of a Second Voyage*, 159, 283, 381.

62 Parry, *Journal of a Second Voyage*, 72.

63 Hall Collection, 58913, book A, 24–5; Parry, *Journal of a Second Voyage*, 384.

64 Hall Collection, 58913, book B, 91.

65 Ibid., book A, 50.

66 Parry, *Journal of a Second Voyage*, illustration titled "Cutting into Winter Island" facing 118.

67 Ibid., 431.

68 Hall Collection, 58913, book A, 16–17; Nourse, *Narrative of the Second Arctic Expedition*, 602.

69 Hall Collection, 58913, book A, 19–22; Nourse, *Narrative of the Second Arctic Expedition*, 602.

70 Hall Collection, 58913, book A, 22–3; Nourse, *Narrative of the Second Arctic Expedition*, 603.

71 Canadian Hydrographic Service chart 7067, 1990.

72 Hall Collection, 58936, 6 April 1868.

73 Hall Collection, 58913, book A, 25; Nourse, *Narrative of the Second Arctic Expedition*, 603.

74 Parry, *Journal of a Second Voyage*, 269, 475.

75 Lyon, *Lyon's Private Journal*, 416.

76 Ibid., 418–19.

77 Ibid., 420–5; Parry, *Journal of a Second Voyage*, 448.

78 Parry, *Journal of a Second Voyage*, 398.

79 Ibid., 227.

80 Cyriax, "Captain Hall and the So-called Survivors," 176.

81 Nourse, *Narrative of the Second Arctic Expedition*, 603.

82 Gilder, *Schwatka's Search*, 79. Some of the Franklin expedition canisters, preserved at the Greenwich Maritime Museum, still show evidence of their red paint. The Inuit also found red-painted cans aboard one of Franklin's abandoned ships.

83 *Historic Tinned Foods*, 61.

84 Ibid., 20.

85 Parry, *Journal of a Second Voyage*, vii, 122.

86 *Historic Tinned Foods*, 29.

87 Hall Collection, 58913, book A, 76–80.

88 Ibid., 81.

89 Hall Collection, 58937, booklet no. 28, 8 May 1869.

90 Parry, *Journal of a Second Voyage*, 214.

91 Ibid., 394–5.

92 Hall Collection, 58937, booklet no. 26, 7 May 1869.

93 Hall Collection, 58913, book A, 75.

94 Parry, *Journal of a Second Voyage*, 274, 478.

95 Hall Collection, 58913, book A, 80.

96 Rae, "Letter of Dr. Rae to the British Admiralty," 285.

97 Hall Collection, 58936, 17 April 1868.

98 Ibid., 19 February 1868.

99 Hall Collection, 58913, book B, 118.

100 Ibid.

101 Ibid., book A, 66–8.

102 Hall Collection, 58936, 8 May 1868.

103 Nourse, *Narrative of the Second Arctic Expedition*, 333.

104 Parry, *Journal of a Second Voyage*, 556.

105 Hall Collection, 58913, book B, 94.

106 Ibid., book A, 49.

107 Ibid., 9.

108 Ibid., 13.

109 Ibid., 22–3; Nourse, *Narrative of the Second Arctic Expedition*, 603.

110 Ibid., book B, 90–1.

111 Ibid., 92–4.

112 Ibid., 95–7.

113 Hall Collection, 58936, 8 April 1868.

114 Hall Collection, 58913, book B, 77–8.

115 Hall Collection, 58933, 74.

116 Hall Collection, 58913, book B, 82–5.

117 Rae, "Letter of Dr. Rae to the British Admiralty," 285.

118 Rae to *New York Herald* dated 23 May and published 4 June 1880.

119 Ibid.

120 Hall Collection, 58936, 8 April 1868.

121 Hall Collection, 58913, book B, 132.

122 Ibid., 128.

123 Hall Collection, 58914, 15 December 1864, 259.

124 Rae, "Letter of Dr. Rae to the British Admiralty," 285–6.

125 Hall Collection, 58933, 38–40.

126 Hall Collection, 58913, book B, 132.

127 Hall Collection, 58916, 13 April 1866.

128 Hall Collection, 58913, book B, 47; 58933, 38–40.

129 Ibid., 285.

130 In an earlier work I concluded that the ship at Ootjoolik was finally abandoned in June/July 1851 and that Aglooka and his men left the care of Tooshooarthariu in the spring of 1852 (Woodman, *Unravelling the Franklin Mystery*, 7, 260).

131 Rae, "Letter of Dr. John Rae to the British Admiralty," 287.

132 Hall Collection, 58936, 19 February 1868.

133 Woodman, *Unravelling the Franklin Mystery*, 7, 260.

CHAPTER THREE

1 Woodman, *Unravelling the Franklin Mystery*, 194ff.

2 Back, *Narrative of Expedition to Mouth of Great Fish River*, 390.

3 Great Britain, Parliamentary Papers, *Accounts and Papers* 41, no. 264 (1847–48).

4 Hall Collection, 58937, booklet no. 38, 18 May 1869.

5 Rasmussen, *Iglulik and Caribou Eskimo Texts*, 92. A nearby encampment called Naujan gave Repulse Bay its modern Inuit name.

6 Nourse, *Narrative of the Second Arctic Expedition*, 590.

7 Ibid., 589.

8 T. Simpson, *Narrative of Discoveries on the North Coast of North America*, 380.

9 Back, *Narrative of Expedition to Mouth of Great Fish River*, 438.

10 Sir John Ross, *Narrative of a Second Voyage in Search of a Northwest Passage*, 2:60.

11 Rae, "Sir John Franklin and His Crews," 15; Rasmussen, *The Netsilik Eskimos*, 84.

12 Mathiassen, *Material Culture of the Iglulik Eskimos*, 27.

13 Lyon, *Lyon's Private Journal*, 53.

14 Rae, *Narrative of an Expedition*, 40.

15 Nourse, *Narrative of the Second Arctic Expedition*, 216–17.

16 Hall Collection, 58926, 203a.

17 Mathiassen, *Material Culture of the Iglulik Eskimos*, 26.

18 Parry, *Journal of a Second Voyage*, 160, 492.

19 Ibid., 89–90.

20 Mathiassen, *Material Culture of the Iglulik Eskimos*, 27.

21 Nourse, *Narrative of the Second Arctic Expedition*, 339.

22 Parry, *Journal of a Second Voyage*, 492.

23 Ibid., 451.

24 Nourse, *Narrative of the Second Arctic Expedition*, 300–1.

25 Ibid., 301–2.

26 Mathiassen, *Material Culture of the Iglulik Eskimos*, 15.

27 Ibid., 21; Damas, *Igluligmiut Kinship and Local Groupings*, 23.

28 Parry, *Journal of a Second Voyage*, 549.

29 Sir John Ross, *Narrative of a Second Voyage in Search of a Northwest Passage*, 109; Woodman, *Unravelling the Franklin Mystery*, 104–5.

30 Cyriax, "Captain Hall and the So-called Survivors of the Franklin Expedition," 172. For a more complete discussion of the Fury Beach cache, see Woodman, *Unravelling the Franklin Mystery*, 104–7.

31 Nourse, *Narrative of the Second Arctic Expedition*, 334.

32 Ibid., 288.

33 Hall Collection, 58937, booklet no. 51, 8 June 1869.

34 Ibid., booklet no. 57, 19 June 1869.

35 Ibid., booklet no. 52, 9 June 1869.

36 Damas, *Igluligmiut Kinship and Local Groupings*, 20–1.

37 Hall Collection, 58915, 346.

38 Rae, "Rae on the Eskimos," 39.

39 Mathiassen, *Material Culture of the Iglulik Eskimos*, 27–8; Nourse, *Narrative of the Second Arctic Expedition*, 63.

40 Bryce, *The Remarkable History of the Hudson's Bay Company*, 374; Tuttle, *Our North Land*, 126–58; Lofthouse, *A Thousand Miles from a Post Office*, 32, 66–69, 107.

41 Ballantyne, *Hudson's Bay*, 137, 23.

42 Birket-Smith, *The Caribou Eskimos*, 167.

43 Ibid.

44 Ibid., 166.

45 Lofthouse, *A Thousand Miles from a Post Office*, 120; Tyrrell, *Across the Sub-Arctics of Canada*.

46 O'Brien, *Alone across the Top of the World*, 222ff.

47 R. Price, *The Howling Arctic*, 73–5.

48 Gilder, *Schwatka's Search*, 3.

49 Ibid., 4.

50 Stackpole, *The Long Arctic Search*, 9–10.

51 Rae, *Narrative of an Expedition*, 75.

52 Rae "Letter of Dr. John Rae to the British Admiralty," 284.

53 Stackpole, *The Long Arctic Search*, 29.

54 Rae, "Letter of Dr. Rae to the British Admiralty," 288.

55 Gilder, *Schwatka's Search*, 15.

56 Ibid., 29–30.

57 Ibid., 38–9.

58 Hall Collection, 58937, booklet no. 22, 2 May 1869.

59 Ibid., booklet no. 38, 18 May 1869; Nourse, *Narrative of the Second Arctic Expedition*, 606; Gilder, *Schwatka's Search*, 90–1; Rasmussen, *The Netsilik Eskimos*, 129.

60 Hall Collection, 58937, booklet no. 38, 18 May 1869, and booklet no. 24, 5 May 1869.

61 Ibid., booklet no. 45, 29 May 1869.

62 Hall Collection, 58926, 22 July 1868.

63 Hall Collection, 58914, 6 December 1864; Nourse, *Narrative of the Second Arctic Expedition*, 64.

64 Hall Collection, 58937, booklet no. 10, April 10 1869.

65 Hall Collection, 58914, 8 December 1864, 216–18.

66 Hall Collection, 58919, 12 July 1866.

67 Nourse, *Narrative of the Second Arctic Expedition*, 591.

68 Ibid.

69 Ibid., 109.

70 Hall Collection, 58914, 8 December 1864, 217.

71 Ibid., 14 December 1864, 251.

72 Gilder, *Schwatka's Search*, 89; Schwatka renders her name as Ahland-nyuck (Stackpole, *The Long Arctic Search*, 62), while Klutschak remembered her as Alañak (Barr *Overland to Starvation Cove*, 73). Hall's Inuit informants called her E-laing-nur.

73 Hall Collection, 58937, booklet no. 38, 18 May 1869.

74 National Archives of Canada, Fairholme Papers, cutting from the *Times* (London), 17 October 1881.

75 Parry, *Journal of a Second Voyage*, 430.

76 Rasmussen, *The Netsilik Eskimos*, 129.

77 Hall Collection, 58937, booklet no. 38, 18 May 1869.

78 Gilder, *Schwatka's Search*, 90–1.

79 Hall Collection, 58937, booklet no. 45, 29 May 1869.

80 Ibid., booklet no. 24, 5 May 1869.

81 Hall Collection, 58914, 14 December 1864, 252.

82 Ibid., 253.

83 Ibid., 252.

84 Parry, *Journal of a Second Voyage*, 503.

85 Ibid., 570, 503; Hall also knew this but apparently never made the connection (see Hall Collection, 58913, book B, 80–2; also 58926, 121).

86 Hall Collection, 58914, 8 December 1864, 218.

87 Hall Collection, 58915, 45.

88 Rae, "Sir John Franklin and His Crews," 14.

89 Hall Collection, 58914, 14 December 1864, 252.

90 Ibid., 6 December 1864.

91 National Archives of Canada, Fairholme Papers, cutting from the *Times* (London), 17 October 1881.

92 Hall Collection, 58919, 4 May 1866.

93 Hall Collection, 58937, booklet no. 45, 29 May 1869.

94 Hall Collection, 58915, 57.

95 Ibid., 65.

96 Ibid., 62.

97 Hall Collection, 58919, 4 May 1866.

98 Hall Collection, 58916a, booklet labelled "May 25–26, 1866."

99 Hall Collection, 58937, booklet no. 38, 18 May 1869.

100 Hall Collection, 58914, 13 December 1864, 242–9; Parry, *Journal of a Second Voyage*, 367.

101 Hall Collection, 58914, 13 December 1864, 242.

102 Ibid., 58919, 12 July 1866.

103 Ibid., 58914, 14 December 1864, 251.

104 Ibid.

105 Ibid.

106 Hall Collection, 58914, 6 December 1864, 210.

107 Ibid., 14 December 1864, 256.

108 This identification was first suggested in 1991; I came upon this confirmation in 1993 (See Woodman, *Unravelling the Franklin Mystery*, 197).

109 Hall Collection, 58914, 13 December 1864, 242, and 14 December 1864, 257.

110 Hall Collection, 58919, 12 July 1866.

111 Owen, *Fate of Franklin*, 233.

112 Hall Collection, 58933, 38.

113 Hall Collection, 58914, 6 December 1864.

114 Ibid.

115 Woodman, *Unravelling the Franklin Mystery*, 241–3.

116 Hall Collection, 58937, booklet no. 28, 7 July 1869.

117 Ibid., booklet no. 31, 11 May 1869; Woodman, *Unravelling the Franklin Mystery*, 165.

118 Wright, *New Light on Franklin*, 78.

119 Ibid., 81.

120 Parry, *Journal of a Second Voyage*, 126.

121 Ibid., 126, xxix; Wright, *New Light on Franklin*, 77–82; Cyriax, "A Note on the Absence of Records," 30–40; Wilkinson, *Arctic Fever*, 102.

122 Markham, *Life of Admiral Sir Leopold McClintock*, 222; Cyriax, *Sir John Franklin's Last Arctic Expedition*, 133.

123 Gilder, *Schwatka's Search*, 147.

124 Hall Collection, 58916a, booklet labelled "May 8–11/66"; Nourse, *Narrative of the Second Arctic Expedition*, 276.

125 For "Shartoo," see Rasmussen, *Netsilik Eskimos*, 18, 22, 100, 104, 112.

126 Hall Collection, 58913, book B, 148.

127 Ibid., 149.

128 A. Simpson, *Life and Travels of Thomas Simpson*, 376.

129 Gibson, "The Dease and Simpson Cairn," 44 (photo).

130 Rae, "The Lost Arctic Voyagers," 435.

131 Rae, "Sir John Franklin and His Crews," 17.

132 Hall Collection, 58937, booklet no. 35, 16 May 1869.

133 Hall Collection, 58913, book B, 154.

134 Hall Collection, 58937, booklet no. 35, 15 May 1869.

135 Ibid., 16 May 1969.

136 Rae, *Narrative of an Expedition*, 106.

137 Ibid., 131.

138 Rae to *New York Herald*, dated 23 May and published 4 July 1880.

139 Hall Collection, 58937, booklet no. 48, 3 June 1869.

140 Ibid., booklet no. 49, 5 June 1869.

141 Nourse, *Narrative of the Second Arctic Expedition*, 109.

142 Ibid., 257.

143 McClintock, *The Voyage of the "Fox,"* 338.

144 Anderson, "Chief Factor James Anderson's Back River Journal of 1855," no. 55, 22.

145 Hall Collection, 58914, 22 December 1864, 284.

146 Hall Collection, 58916a, booklet no. 8, 13 April 1866.

147 Nourse, *Narrative of the Second Arctic Expedition*, 257.

148 Hall Collection, 58913, book A, 47.

149 Hall Collection, 58914, 15 December 1864, 258–60; Nourse, *Narrative of the Second Arctic Expedition*, 593–4. "Kinnapatoo" is not a true determinative for these Inuit, who more properly belong to the Qaernermiut (see Eber, *When the Whalers Were Up North*, 131).

150 Hall Collection, 58914, 14 December 1864, 252–3.

151 Ibid., 8 December 1864, 219.

152 Ibid., 15 December 1864, 260–1.

153 Hall Collection, 58915, 351–2.

154 Rae to *New York Herald* dated 23 May 1880, published 4 July 1880.

155 Rae, *Doctor John Rae's Correspondence*, xxviii, lxxviii.

156 Hall Collection, 58914, 15 December 1864, 260–1.

157 Ibid.

158 Hall Collection, 58933, 142.

CONCLUSION

1 Hall Collection, 58913, book A, 39–40.

2 Nourse, *Narrative of the Second Arctic Expedition*, 334.

3 Ibid., 339.

4 Hall Collection, 58936, 9 May 1868.

5 Cyriax, "Captain Hall and the So-called Survivors," 184.

6 Loomis, *Weird and Tragic Shores*, 213–14.

7 Woodman, *Unravelling the Franklin Mystery*, 270.

8 Ibid.

9 Nourse, *Narrative of the Second Arctic Expedition*, 339.

Bibliography

UNPUBLISHED SOURCES

MUSEUM OF ARMED FORCES HISTORY, NAVAL HISTORY SECTION, SMITHSONIAN INSTITUTION, WASHINGTON
No. 2157, Hall Collection
The Hall Collection of journals, notebooks, letters, and artifacts is extensive and unindexed. While its custodians have made a commendable effort to arrange it in some logical fashion, they have been hampered by Hall's work habits and the fact that portions of his material were taken to the Arctic on his third expedition and never returned.

Of primary interest are the contents of Hall's original pencilled notebooks, much of which he later transcribed (with additions and corrections) into various journals. Also of value are two transcriptions of the relevant material that were made for the benefit of Franklin's widow, at Hall's direction, by his friend John Copp (58913-N, books A and B). The information provided below should allow the original documents to be located. Where the documents have numbered pages, I have included the page numbers in the notes; where they do not, I have given the dates under which portions were written.

58909-N (no. 1) Rough journal, 1 May 1863 to 4 September 1864
58911-N (no. 3) Journal for August and October 1864
58912-N (no. 4) Rough notes and letter, August 1864

58913-N (no. 5) Two books marked "A" and "B"

58914-N (no. 6) Journal, December 1864 to May 1865

58915-N (no. 7) Journal, November 1865 to April 1866

58916-N (no. 8) Two packages of rough notes ("a" and "b"), March to June 1866 (21 notebooks)

58919-N (no. 11) Journal from May 1866 to 14 July 1866

58922-N (no. 14) Nine packages of loose notes and papers

58926-N (no. 18) Journal, 4 August 1866 to 26 September 1869

58930-N (no. 25) Journal, 14 to 23 May 1865

58933-N (no. 28) Private journal, April 1868–69; "Sir John Franklin" book

58936-N (no. 31) Rough notes, February to June 1868 (41 booklets)

58937-N (no. 32) Rough notes, 21 March to 20 June 1869 (58 booklets)

58939-N (no. 34) Rough notes, August to November 1864

58943-N (no. 38) Miscellaneous correspondence after return from second Arctic expedition

AMERICAN MUSEUM OF NATURAL HISTORY, WASHINGTON
Comer Papers, Journal no. 8

HUDSON'S BAY COMPANY ARCHIVES, WINNIPEG
E 15/3, 15/8, 15/9, Rae expeditions
E 15/4, Franklin expedition

NATIONAL ARCHIVES OF CANADA, OTTAWA
Fairholme Papers 1834–45, notebook labelled "Letters and Journals W.F., G.F., J.F."

NATIONAL MARITIME MUSEUM, GREENWICH, ENGLAND
Arctic Collection, doc. 2/121.

PUBLIC RECORD OFFICE, LONDON, ENGLAND
ADM 1/1582, George Back expedition
ADM 7/187, Franklin expedition
ADM 37/6669, 6689, muster books of *Fury* and *Hecla*
ADM 38/9162, 1962, muster books of *Terror*
ADM 38/8045, 672, muster books of *Erebus*

ROYAL GEOGRAPHICAL SOCIETY ARCHIVES, LONDON, ENGLAND
Cyriax Papers, 1(b), "Notes on *Quest for Franklin*"

Bibliography

SCOTT POLAR RESEARCH INSTITUTE, CAMBRIDGE, ENGLAND
MS 248/303, John Franklin letters
MS 787/1, Rae autobiography

PUBLISHED SOURCES

Anderson, James. *The Hudson Bay Expedition in Search of Sir John Franklin.* Toronto: Canadiana House 1969.

Back, George. *Narrative of the Arctic Land Expedition to the Mouth of the Great Fish River.* London: John Murray 1836. Reprint, Edmonton: Hurtig 1970.

Balikci, Asen. *The Netsilik Eskimo.* Garden City, N.Y.: Natural History Press 1970.

Ballantyne, R.M. *Hudson's Bay, or Everyday Life in the Wilds of North America.* 2d ed. Edinburgh: Blackwood 1848.

Barr, William. *Overland to Starvation Cove: With the Inuit in Search of Franklin, 1878–1880.* Toronto: University of Toronto Press 1987.

Birket-Smith, Kaj. *The Caribou Eskimos: Material and Social Life and Their Cultural Position.* Report of the Fifth Thule Expedition, 1921–24, vol. 5. Copenhagen: Glydensdalke Boghandel, Nordisk Forlag 1929. Reprint, New York: AMS Press 1976.

Bryce, George. *The Remarkable History of the Hudson's Bay Company.* New York: Burt Franklin 1968.

Bunyan, Ian, et al. *No Ordinary Journey: John Rae Arctic Explorer 1813–93.* Edinburgh: National Museums of Scotland 1993.

Cyriax, R.J. *Sir John Franklin's Last Arctic Expedition.* London: Methuen 1939.

– "Captain Hall and the So-called Survivors of the Franklin Expedition." *Polar Record* 4 (1944): 170–85.

– "Recently Discovered Traces of Sir John Franklin's Expedition." *Geographical Journal* 117 (June 1951): 211–14.

– "The Two Franklin Expedition Records Found on King William Island." *Mariner's Mirror* 44 (1958): 179–89.

– "A Note on the Absence of Records." *Scottish Geographical Magazine* 75, no. 1 (1959): 30–40.

Damas, David. *Igluligmiut Kinship and Local Groupings: A Structural Approach.* Ottawa: Department of Northern Affairs and National Resources 1963.

Dease, Peter Warren, and Thomas Simpson. "Narrative of the Progress of Arctic Discoveries on the Northern Shore of America, in the Summer of 1839." *Royal Geographical Society Journal* 10 (1841): 268–74.

Eber, Dorothy Harley. *When the Whalers Were Up North: Inuit Memories From the Eastern Arctic.* Montreal: McGill-Queen's University Press 1989.

Fitzjames, James. "Journal of James Fitzjames aboard Erebus, 1845." *Nautical Magazine and Naval Chronicle* 21 (1852): 158–65, 195–201.

Fluhmann, May. *Second in Command: Life of F.R.M. Crozier.* Yellowknife: Northwest Territories, Department of Information 1976.

Francis, Daniel. *Arctic Chase.* St John's, Nfld: Breakwater Books 1984.

Gibson, William. "The Dease and Simpson Cairn." *Beaver* 264 (September 1933): 44–5.

Gilder, William H. *Schwatka's Search: Sledging in the Arctic in Quest of Franklin Records.* New York: Charles Scribner 1881.

Great Britain. Parliamentary Papers, Arctic Exploration.

– "Further Papers Relative to the Recent Arctic Expeditions in Search of Sir John Franklin and the Crews of the Erebus and Terror." House of Commons Sessional Papers, *Accounts and Papers* 35, no. 1898 (1854–55).

– "Further Papers Relative to the Recent Arctic Expeditions in Search of Sir John Franklin and the Crews of the Erebus and Terror." House of Commons Sessional Papers, *Accounts and Papers* 41, no. 2124 (1856).

Hall, Charles Francis. *Life with the Esquimaux: A Narrative of Arctic Experience in Search of Survivors of Sir John Franklin's Expedition.* London: Sampson, Low, and Marston 1862. Reprint, Edmonton: Hurtig 1970.

Hearne, Samuel. *A Journey from Prince of Wales's Fort in Hudson's Bay to the Northern Ocean.* Reprint, Toronto: Macmillan 1958.

Historic Tinned Foods. Pamphlet no. 85. Greenford, Middlesex: International Tin Research and Development Corporation 1939.

Jones, A.G.E. "Rear Admiral Sir William Edward Parry: A Different View." *Musk-Ox* 21 (1978): 3–10.

Lofthouse, J. *A Thousand Miles from a Post Office, or Twenty Years' Life and Travels in the Hudson's Bay Regions.* London: Society for Promoting Christian Knowledge 1922.

Loomis, Chauncey C. *Weird and Tragic Shores.* New York: Knopf 1971.

Lubbock, A. Basil. *The Arctic Whalers.* Glasgow: Brown and Ferguson 1937.

Lyon, G. *Lyon's Private Journal.* London: John Murray 1824.

McClintock, Francis Leopold. *The Voyage of the "Fox" in the Arctic Seas: A Narrative of the Discovery of the Fate of Sir John Franklin and His Companions.* Philadelphia: Porter and Coates 1859. Reprint, Edmonton: Hurtig 1972.

– "Discoveries by the Late Expedition in Search of Sir John Franklin and His Party." *Royal Geographical Society Proceedings* 4 (1859): 2–13.

MacKay, Douglas. *The Honourable Company.* London: Cassell 1937.

Mangles, James, ed. *Papers and Despatches relating to the Arctic Searching Expeditions of 1850–51–52.* 2d ed. London: Francis and John Rivington 1852.

Markham, C.R. *Life of Admiral Sir Leopold McClintock.* London 1909.

Mathiassen, Therkel. *Material Culture of the Iglulik Eskimos.* Report of the Fifth Thule Expedition, 1921–24, vol. 7, no. 1. Copenhagen: Glydensdalke Boghandel, Nordisk Forlag 1928. Reprint, New York: AMS Press 1976.

Neatby, L.H. *Search for Franklin.* New York: Walker 1970.

– "Joe and Hannah." *Beaver* 290 (autumn 1969): 16–21.

Nourse, J.E., ed. *Narrative of the Second Arctic Expedition Commanded by Charles Francis Hall.* Washington: Government Printing Office 1879.

O'Brien, Jack. *Alone across the Top of the World.* Chicago: John C. Winston 1935.

Osborn, Sherard. *Stray Leaves from an Arctic Journal.* London: Longman, Brown, Green, and Longmans 1852.

Oswalt, Wendell H. *Eskimos and Explorers.* Novato, Calif.: Chandler and Sharp 1979.

Owen, Roderick. *Fate of Franklin.* London: Hutchinson 1978.

Parry, Ann. *Parry of the Arctic.* London: Chatto and Windus 1963.

Parry, Edward. *Memoirs of Rear Admiral Sir W. Edward Parry, Kt.* London: Longman, Brown, Green, Longmans, and Roberts 1857.

Parry, William Edward. *Journal of a Second Voyage for the Discovery of a Northwest Passage ... performed in the Years 1821–22–23 in H.M.S. "Fury" and "Hecla."* London: John Murray 1824. Reprint, New York: Greenwood Press 1969.

Price, Ray. *The Howling Arctic.* Toronto: Peter Martin 1970.

Rae, John. *Narrative of an Expedition to the Shores of the Arctic Sea in 1846 and 1847.* London: John Murray 1850. Reprint, Toronto: Canadiana House 1970.

– "The Lost Arctic Voyagers." *Household Words,* 23 December 1854, 433–7.

– "Sir John Franklin and His Crews." *Household Words,* 3 February 1855, 12–20.

– "On the Esquimaux." *Transactions of the Ethnological Society of London* 4 (1866): 138–53.

– "Letter of Dr. John Rae to the British Admiralty." *American Geographical Society of New York Journal* 12 (1880): 284–8.

– "Arctic Exploration." *New York Herald,* 4 July 1880.

– *Doctor John Rae's Correspondence with the Hudson's Bay Company on Arctic Exploration 1844–55,* ed. E.E. Rich and A.M. Johnson, with introduction by J.M. Wordie and R.J. Cyriax. London: Hudson's Bay Record Society 1953.

Bibliography

– "Rae on the Eskimos." *Beaver* 284 (March 1954): 38–41.

Rasmussen, Knud, J. *Intellectual Culture of the Iglulik Eskimos.* Report of the Fifth Thule Expedition, 1921–24, vol. 7, no. 1. Copenhagen: Glydensdalke Boghandel, Nordisk Forlag 1929. Reprint, New York: AMS Press 1976.

– *Observations on the Intellectual Culture of the Caribou Eskimos.* Report of the Fifth Thule Expedition, 1921–24, vol. 7, no. 2. Copenhagen: Glydensdalke Boghandel, Nordisk Forlag 1930. Reprint, New York: AMS Press 1976.

– *Iglulik and Caribou Eskimo Texts.* Report of the Fifth Thule Expedition, 1921–24, vol. 7, no. 3. Copenhagen: Glydensdalke Boghandel, Nordisk Forlag 1930. Reprint, New York: AMS Press 1976.

– *The Netsilik Eskimos.* Report of the Fifth Thule Expedition, 1921–24, vol. 8, no. 1–2. Copenhagen: Glydensdalke Boghandel, Nordisk Forlag 1931. Reprint, New York: AMS Press 1976.

Ross, Sir John. *Narrative of a Second Voyage in Search of a North West Passage, and of a Residence in the Arctic Regions during the Years 1829–30–31–32–33; with Appendix.* 2 vols. London: A.W. Webster 1835.

Ross, W. Gillies. *Whaling and Eskimos: Hudson Bay 1860–1915.* Ottawa: National Museum of Man 1975.

Simpson, Alexander. *Life and Travels of Thomas Simpson.* London: Richard Bentley 1845.

Simpson, Thomas. *Narrative of Discoveries on the North Coast of North America during the Years 1836–39.* London: Richard Bentley 1843.

Stackpole, E.A., ed. *The Long Arctic Search.* Chester, Conn.: Pequot Press 1977.

Starbuck, Alexander. *A History of American Whale Fishery.* New York: Argosy Antiquarian 1964.

Stefansson, Vilhjalmur. "Rae's Arctic Correspondence." *Beaver* 284 (March 1954): 36–7.

Tuttle, Charles R. *Our North Land: Being a Full Account of the Canadian North-West and Hudson's Bay Route.* Toronto: C. Blackett Robinson 1885.

Tyrrell, J.W. *Across the Sub-Arctics of Canada.* London: T. Fisher Unwin 1898. Reprint, Toronto: Coles 1973.

Wallace, R.C. "Rae of the Arctic." *Beaver* 284 (March 1954): 28–33.

Wilkinson, Douglas. *Arctic Fever.* Toronto: Clarke Irwin 1971.

Woodman, David C. *Unravelling the Franklin Mystery: Inuit Testimony.* Montreal: McGill-Queen's University Press 1991.

Wright, Noel. *New Light on Franklin.* Ipswich: W.J. Cowell 1949.

– *Quest for Franklin.* London: Heinemann 1959.

Index

Index

Index